Table of Contents

UNIT 1: Lent

UNIT 2: Holy Week

UNIT 3: Proclaim

Please adjust this schedule to fit your church's needs.

Find all kinds of cool stuff at our website. Just go to: www.cokesburykids.com

Here's How the Reproducible Kids' Book Works

Celebrate Wonder All Ages resources are designed for children ages 3–12 to learn together. The Leader Guide includes suggestions for both group activities and individual activities. Some of the activities use reproducible sheets from this book.

Reproducible sheets are labeled at the top. Choose the activities that will work best for your group. Simply tear out the sheets you want to use; they are perforated in the center. Then photocopy the sheets you need for each child.

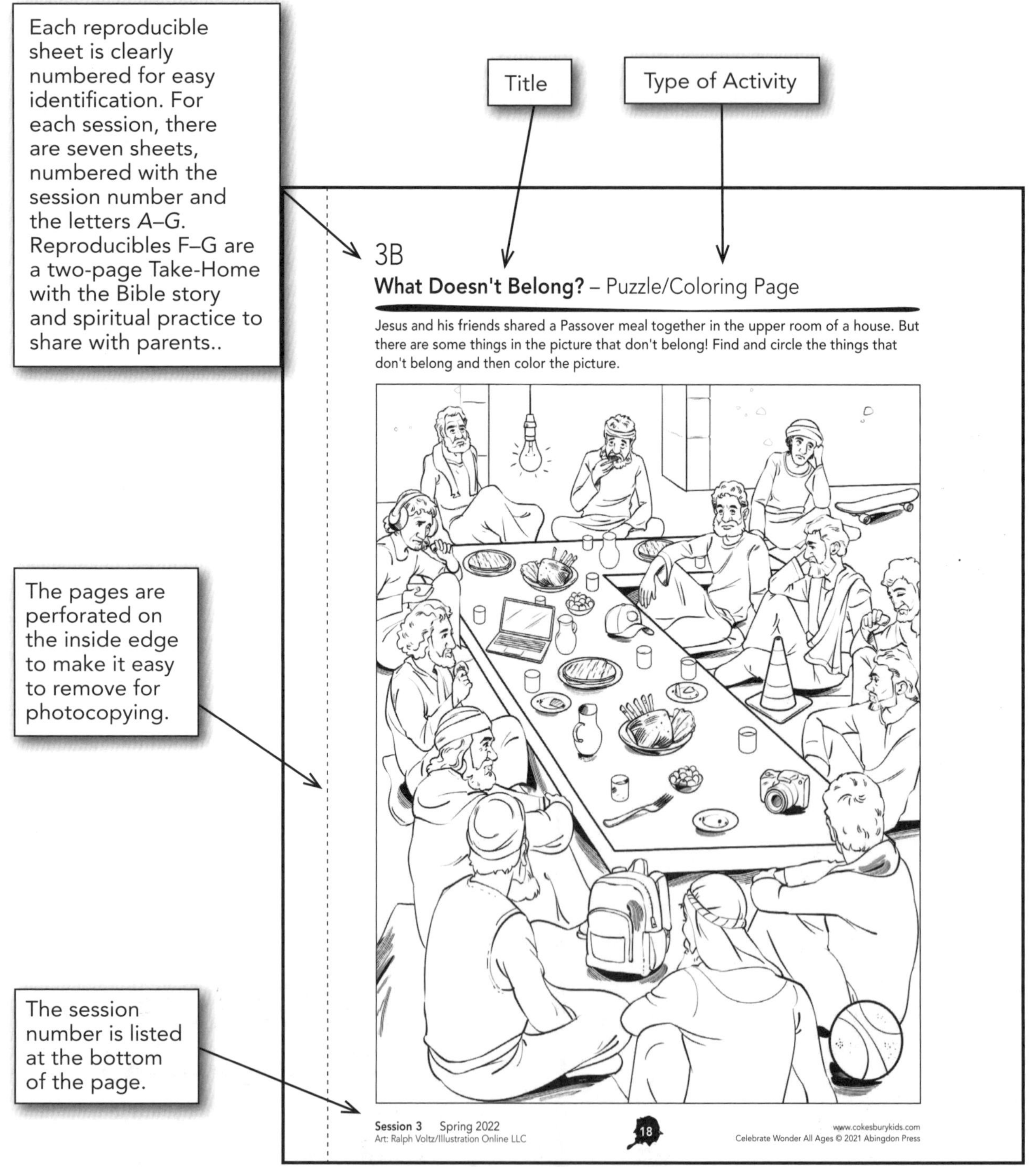

1A

Ten Men with Skin Disease – Coloring Page

Ten men had gotten sick and were not allowed to live with their families anymore. They heard Jesus could heal people, so they called out to him. What do you think happened next?

Art: Tatevik Avakyan/Illustration Online LLC

1B

Ten Men to the Priests – Maze

Ten men with skin diseases met Jesus and asked him to heal them. Jesus told them to go to the priests. During Jesus' time, priests were the ones who could admit people back into their communities. By sending them to see the priests, Jesus was saying they could go back home because they were healed.

1C

Who is Missing? – Draw and Color Page

Ten men with skin diseases called out to Jesus for help. They wanted to be healed so they could return home. Draw the four missing men and then color the picture.

1D

Accessibility Audit – Inclusion Activity

Ten men with skin diseases were excluded from their community. Are there people who might not be able to be a part of your church community because there isn't safe access for them? Look around your church and see what might be keeping people from church.

	YES	NO
1. Does your church have ramps that lead into the building?	☐	☐
2. Are there clear signs that mark the entrances?	☐	☐
3. Are there doors wide enough for people in wheelchairs?	☐	☐
4. Are there parking spots close to the building for people with disabilities?	☐	☐
5. Are the entrance door frames flat?	☐	☐
6. Do the entrance doors have automatic openers?	☐	☐
7. Are there clear signs that help people find where they want to go?	☐	☐
8. Are the hallways at least 36" wide?	☐	☐
9. If your church has more than one floor, does your church have an elevator?	☐	☐
10. Can you open all the doors with one hand?	☐	☐
11. Do the fire alarms make loud noises and flash bright lights?	☐	☐
12. Are sinks easy to reach?	☐	☐
13. Are water fountains easy to reach?	☐	☐
14. Are there spaces in the pews for people in wheelchairs?	☐	☐
15. Is the choir area accessible to people in wheelchairs?	☐	☐
16. Is fellowship time held in a location that everyone can access?	☐	☐
17. Are the colors used easy to see by people who are colorblind?	☐	☐
18. Are there braille documents available?	☐	☐
19. Are service animals welcome?	☐	☐
20. Is there an American Sign Language interpreter?	☐	☐

1E

Lenten Calendar – At-Home Activity

Lent is a church season that lasts from Ash Wednesday until Easter. It's forty days, excluding Sundays, of reflection and growing closer to God in preparation of Easter. Use this countdown calendar to track Lent together as a family.

Lenten Calendar 2022

Sunday	Monday	Tuesday	Wednesday	Thursday	Friday	Saturday
			2 Ash Wednesday MARCH	3	4	5
6 Mini Easter	7	8	9	10	11	12
13 Mini Easter	14	15	16	17	18	19
20 Mini Easter	21	22	23	24	25	26
27 Mini Easter	28	29	30	31	1 APRIL	2
3 Mini Easter	4	5	6	7	8	9
10 Mini Easter	11	12	13	14 Holy Thursday	15 Good Friday	16 Holy Saturday
17 **EASTER**						

Art: Shutterstock

1F

Ten Men with Skin Disease – Luke 17:11-19

Jesus was on his way to the city of Jerusalem. Along the way, he came upon a small village. As he passed through, ten men approached him.

Keeping their distance, the ten men shouted, "Jesus, please help us!"

Jesus turned and looked closely at the men. The ten men had skin diseases. They looked like their skin hurt and itched. They looked lonely and sad and tired. Jesus knew that the men weren't allowed to be with their families and friends because they were sick. The men had to quarantine to keep from spreading the sickness to the people they loved.

But Jesus didn't want them to be sick and alone. Jesus said, "Go see the priests! They will see that you are well again and you will be allowed to rejoin your families."

The ten men were suprised and took off running toward their homes. As they ran, they were healed.

One of the men looked down and noticed his skin had been healed. He shouted, "Praise God! I am healed!" He turned back to Jesus.

When he got back to Jesus he fell down at Jesus' feet and said, "Thank you, Jesus!"

Jesus looked at the man, a Samaritan. Jesus asked, "Weren't there ten of you who were healed? But only you, someone who is a different ethnicity than me, came back to say thank you. Wow! Your faith has healed you."

Family Spiritual Practice **Bible Passage:** Luke 17:11-19

Wonder: After reading the story from the Bible or from the *Celebrate Wonder Bible Storybook*, wonder together. **Ask:** What are you thankful for?

Do: This Wednesday marks the start of Lent. Use the Lenten Countdown Calendar by marking off each day until Easter.

Pray: Dear God, thank you for community and family and friends. Amen.

1G

Feeling God's Presence

Draw a place where you feel God's presence the most in the space below. If you can, go and spend time in this place this week.

2A

A Blind Man Is Healed – Coloring Page

A man who was blind called out to Jesus and asked Jesus to heal him. He wanted to see. Jesus spoke and the man could see!

Art: Tatevik Avakyan/Illustration Online LLC

2B

Hidden Word – Coloring Page and Puzzle

A man asked Jesus to help him see. Jesus gave him back his sight. What do you think the man did in response to his healing? Find the hidden letters to find out!

______ ______ ______ ______ ______ ______

2C

Missing Vowels – Puzzle

This month's Bible verse comes from Luke 11:9. The words below are missing their vowels. Add the correct vowels to each word to complete this month's memory verse.

2D

Lenten Wonder Cube – Home Activity

Lent is the church season where Christians prepare their hearts for Easter for forty days. Use this Lenten Wonder Cube with your family as a way to help you prepare.

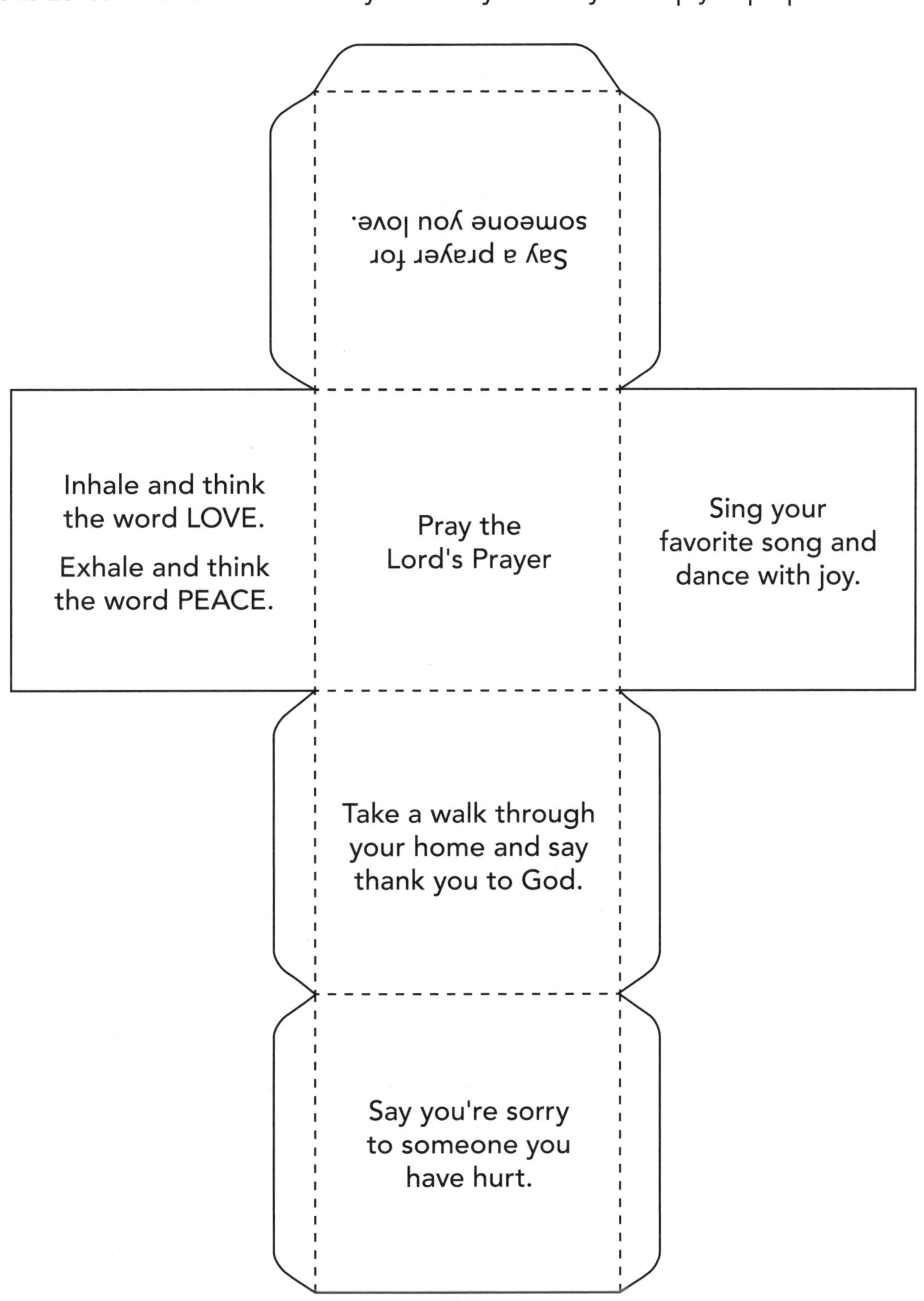

Art: Shutterstock

2E

Binoculars – Art Activity

The man in our story wanted to see. When you look around, what do you see?

2F

A Blind Man Is Healed – Luke 18:35-43

A man was sitting on the side of the road asking for help. He was blind—he couldn't see anything. Because he couldn't see, he couldn't work. So, each day he sat by the road hoping someone would give him money or food.

This particular day, as the man sat on the side of the road, he heard lots of noise headed his way. He heard the sounds of lots of feet walking and lots of people talking. It sounded like a big crowd was walking down the road. Then the man heard someone say the name "Jesus."

"Hey!" the man shouted, "what is happening?"

"Jesus is walking this way," said someone in the crowd.

Without any hesitation, the man because calling out to Jesus. The people in the crowd told him to be quiet. This only made the man yell louder.

"Jesus, Son of David, please show me mercy!" the man yelled.

Over all of the noise, Jesus heard the man's call. Jesus stopped, scanned the crowd, and asked someone to bring the man to him.

The people in the crowd helped the man get to Jesus.

Jesus asked the man, "What do you want me to do for you?"

The man said, "Lord, I want to see."

Jesus said, "Receive your sight! Your faith has healed you."

All at once, the man was able to see! He began praising God, and all the people in the crowd began praising God too.

Family Spiritual Practice

Bible Passage: Luke 18:35-43

Wonder: After reading the story from the Bible or from the *Celebrate Wonder Bible Storybook*, wonder together. **Ask:** What would you ask Jesus to do for you?

Do: This week, use your Lenten Wonder Cube together during bedtime.

Pray: Dear God, thank you for listening to our hearts' desires. Amen.

2G

What do you pray for?

The man who was blind knew what he really wanted from Jesus—to see. What do you pray the hardest for? Draw or write about it.

The Last Supper – Coloring Page

Jesus and his friends travelled to the city of Jerusalem to celebrate the Festival of Passover. They shared this special meal together.

Art: Tatevik Avakyan/Illustration Online LLC

3B

What Doesn't Belong? – Puzzle/Coloring Page

Jesus and his friends shared a Passover meal together in the upper room of a house. But there are some things in the picture that don't belong! Find and circle the things that don't belong and then color the picture.

3C

Scrambled Story – Puzzle

In today's Bible story, Jesus shares the Passover meal with his disciples. Below, you will find some of the words found in today's Bible passage. Unscramble them to learn more about today's story. You can look up the passage (Matthew 26:17-35) if you need help.

lneeeUadnv _ _ _ _ _ _ _ _ _ _

spiDclise _ _ _ _ _ _ _ _ _

vsesPrao _ _ _ _ _ _ _ _

nivEeng _ _ _ _ _ _ _

daeSednd _ _ _ _ _ _ _ _

sdelsBe _ _ _ _ _ _ _

vCeanont _ _ _ _ _ _ _ _

3D

Jesus' Words – Art Activity

Jesus blessed and broke a loaf of bread and gave it to his friends saying, "Remember me." When we gather for Communion, we remember Jesus and his words from this story.

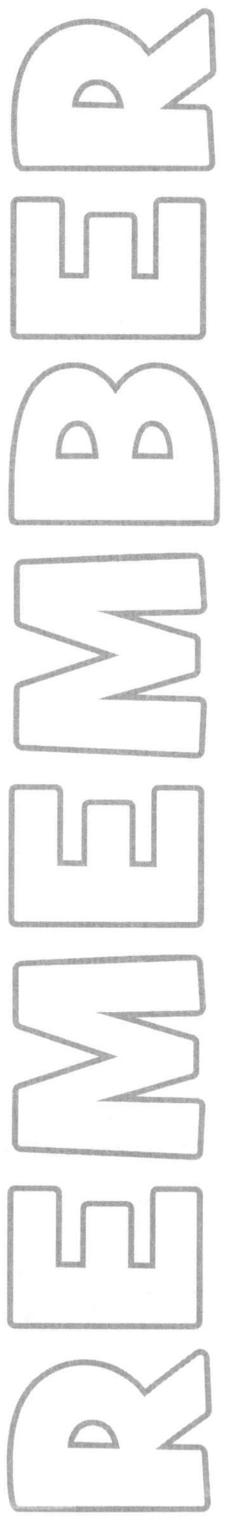

3E

Unleavened Bread – Intergenerational Activity

Follow the recipe to make unleavened bread.

Unleavened Bread

Ingredients:

2 cups whole wheat flour

1 Tbsp. sugar

1 tsp. salt

2 Tbsp. olive oil

1 cup water

Directions:

Preheat oven to 400 degrees.

Spray a baking sheet with cooking spray.

Combine all ingredients in a mixing bowl. Stir well.

Place the dough on a floured work surface. Knead the dough for several minutes. Divide dough into 12 pieces.

Use your hands to shape each piece of dough into a circle and flatten it onto the prepared baking sheet.

Use a fork to prick holes over the surface of each bread piece.

Bake bread at 400 degrees for 10 minutes.

3F

The Last Supper – Matthew 26:17-35

Every year, the Jewish people celebrate a special festival called Passover. They gather with family and friends to celebrate the time when God saved the people from slavery in Egypt. Because Jesus was Jewish, every year he celebrated Passover.

In the last year of Jesus's life, Jesus was in Jerusalem with his friends, the disciples. They asked Jesus where he wanted to have the Passover meal. Jesus told them to go into the city. "There will be a certain man. Tell him that my time is near and that we want to celebrate Passover at his house."

The disciples listened to Jesus' and found the man. Then they prepared the Passover meal.

That night, everyone came together to celebrate Passover and eat the special meal.

During the meal, Jesus said, "One of you is going to betray me. You are going to have me arrested."

The disciples were shocked and sad. How could this be?

Jesus said, "There are stories about the savior and his death. But it still upsets me."

Judas looked uneasy. "Is it me?" he asked.

Jesus looked at Judas, "You said it."

Everyone was uneasy and sad. Was this really the last time they'd be sharing this special meal together?

Then Jesus took the bread, blessed it, broke it, and shared it. "Every time you eat bread, remember me." He then took a cup of juice, thanked God for it, and shared it. "This is the cup of the new covenant. Every time you drink juice, remember me."

After the meal, they sang songs of praise and walked to the Mount of Olives.

Family Spiritual Practice **Bible Passage:** Matthew 26:17-35

Wonder: After reading the story from the Bible or from the *Celebrate Wonder Bible Storybook*, wonder together. **Ask:** What do you remember about the stories of Jesus?

Do: This week, turn off your devices each night at dinner. Use this time to connect with each other and with God.

Pray: Dear God, thank you for the special meals we share with each other. Amen.

3G
Favorite Meal

What's your favorite special meal? Draw it below.

4A

In the Garden – Coloring Page

After the Passover meal, Jesus and his friends went to the garden of Gethsemane, a special place for Jesus. Jesus said prayers to God in the garden and shared his sadness with God.

4B

Match the Flowers – Puzzle

Jesus prayed to God in the garden of Gethsemane. Draw a line to the matching flowers and plants.

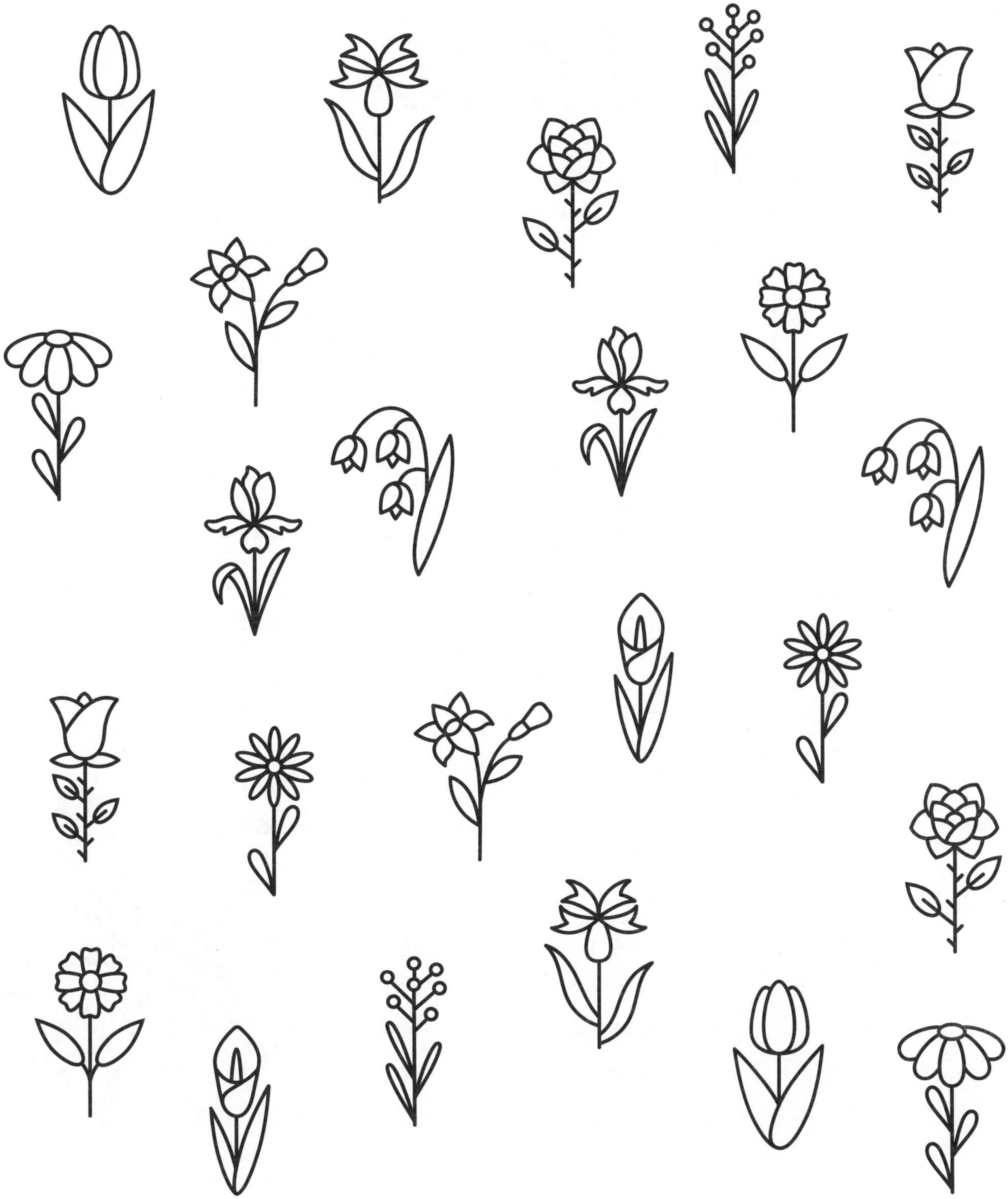

4C

Lenten Word Search – Puzzle

This month we have heard stories about the last days of Jesus' life. We hear these stories each year during the church season of Lent. Use the word bank to find and circle words from this month's stories.

Lent

D	W	C	F	W	X	W	E	E	F	Z	W
D	B	L	I	N	D	F	N	L	X	X	K
G	S	K	I	N	D	I	S	E	A	S	E
A	C	O	M	M	U	N	I	T	Y	Z	Q
R	S	E	E	R	H	E	A	L	R	E	V
D	O	Q	Y	Y	N	W	U	P	E	N	O
E	V	A	R	M	S	Q	U	J	M	M	P
N	R	J	E	R	I	C	H	O	E	L	C
P	A	S	S	O	V	E	R	D	M	B	O
X	C	T	B	B	R	E	A	D	B	P	S
R	G	J	E	R	U	S	A	L	E	M	M
I	Q	X	X	N	J	B	M	J	R	C	R

blind	heal	remember
bread	Jericho	sad
community	Jerusalem	see
cup	Passover	skin disease
garden	pray	ten

4D

March Stars and Constellations – Home Activity

Stars move across the sky and change each season. Constellations and asterisms are star pictures made from groupings of stars. The star pictures below can be found this month by facing south.

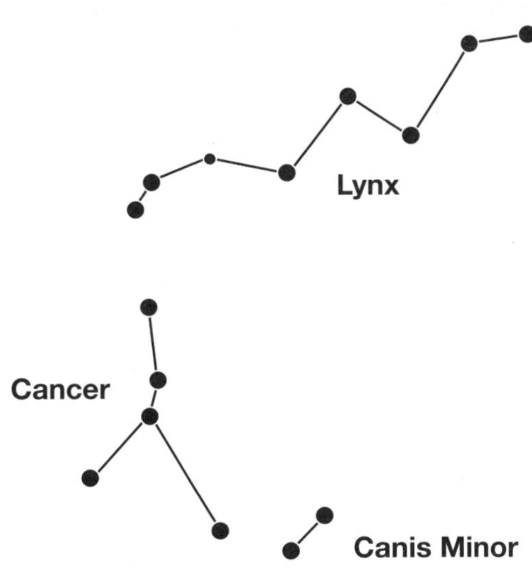

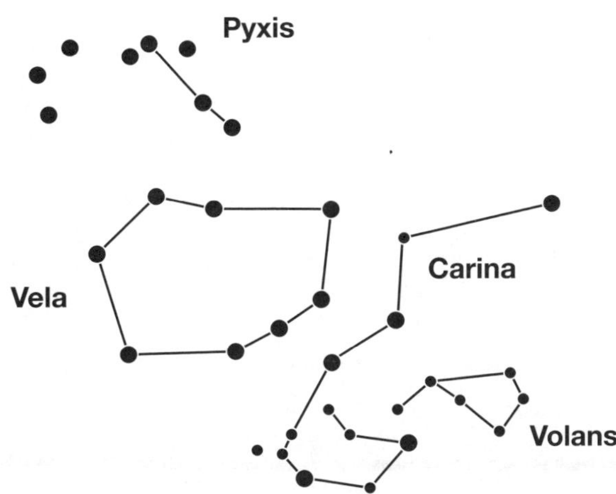

4E

Feelings in the Garden – Art Activity

There are lots of feelings in today's Bible story. Draw or paint a portrait of yourself feeling one of the feelings from the story.

AFRAID SAD ANNOYED WORRIED SLEEPY COMFORTED

Art: Shutterstock

4F

In the Garden – Matthew 26:36-46

After the Passover meal, Jesus and the disciples walked to the garden of Gethsemane. It was the middle of the night, but Jesus needed some space to pray to God.

When they got to the garden, Jesus asked Peter, James, and John to come with him. He asked the rest of the disciples to wait at the front of the garden.

Jesus, Peter, James, and John walked farther into the garden. Jesus turned to his closest friends and said, "I am very sad, so sad it's like I am dying. Please stay here and keep watch with me while I pray." They agreed to keep watch and Jesus walked farther into the garden.

Jesus fell onto his face and prayed to God, "Father, please take away my pain. But if you can't, I will do what you want."

Jesus got up and walked back to Peter, James, and John. They were asleep and not keeping watch. "Wake up! Couldn't you stay awake while I prayed? Stay awake while I pray some more."

Jesus walked back into the garden and prayed, "Abba, Dad, please take away my pain. But if you can't, I will do what you want."

Jesus's friends had fallen back asleep, so he went back to praying.

Jesus prayed again, "Father, please take away my pain. But if you can't, I will do what you want."

Jesus went back to his disciples and told them to wake up. It was time for Jesus' arrest.

Family Spiritual Practice   Bible Passage: Matthew 26:36-46

Wonder: After reading the story from the Bible or from the *Celebrate Wonder Bible Storybook*, wonder together. **Ask:** What do you remember about the stories of Jesus?

Do: This week, turn off your devices each night at dinner. Use this time to connect with each other and with God.

Pray: Dear God, thank you for the special meals we share with each other. Amen.

4G

Prayer Labyrinth

Jesus walked into the garden and prayed. Then he walked back out prepared to do whatever God needed him to do. Christians created prayer labyrinths to help us do the same. Use your finger to slowly trace the path to the center. Say a prayer, then trace the path back out.

5A

Peter's Denial – Coloring Page

Jesus was arrested and was accused of doing bad things even though he hadn't. Peter was in the courtyard waiting to see what would happen to Jesus. Some people asked him if he was friends with Jesus. What do you think he told them?

5B

Peter's Rooster – Color by Number

Jesus told Peter that Peter would deny knowing him three times by the time the rooster crowed. What do you think Peter did?

1=Yellow
2=Orange
3=Red
4=Brown
5=Black
6=Blue

5C

Spring Coded Message – Puzzle

In today's Bible story, Peter is asked if he knows Jesus. Use the flower code below to find out what Peter said.

5D

Monthly Memory Verse – Puzzle

Cut out the puzzle pieces and then put the puzzle together to learn this month's memory verse.

5E

Learning From Mistakes – Social-Emotional Activity

In our Bible story, Peter makes a mistake! We will hear a story in a few weeks about what he learns from this mistake. We all make mistakes and they give us a chance to learn and do better next time.

5F

Peter's Denial – Matthew 26:69-75

While Jesus prayed in the garden, a crowd came and arrested him. There were people who wanted Jesus to get into trouble for all of the things he was teaching about God. The crowd took him to the person who decided what to do with troublemakers, the high priest. Peter followed the crowd to see what would happen to Jesus.

While Jesus was being questioned by the high priest, Peter stood in a courtyard. Peter tried to blend in. But a woman saw him and said, "You were with Jesus."

"No, I wasn't with Jesus," replied Peter.

Peter moved to a different spot in the courtyard and tried not to draw any attention to himself. But another woman saw Peter and said, "You were with Jesus."

"No, I don't know that person! I wasn't with Jesus!" Peter shouted.

Peter again tried to blend in, but the people there said, "You talk like someone from Galilee. You have a Galilean accent. You must be one of Jesus' friends."

Peter shouted loudly, "I DO NOT KNOW HIM!"

Just then a rooster crowed.

Peter remembered what Jesus had said, "Peter you will deny knowing me three times before the rooster crows."

Peter burst into tears and ran out of the courtyard while he cried deeply.

Family Spiritual Practice **Bible Passage:** Matthew 26:69-75

Wonder: After reading the story from the Bible or from the *Celebrate Wonder Bible Storybook,* wonder together. **Ask:** What part of this story do you wonder about?

Do: Practice a growth mindset this week. What things are you still learning?

Pray: Dear God, we will make mistakes. Thank you for showing us love and grace while we learn. Amen.

5G

Feelings of Guilt

Do you wonder why Peter said he wasn't friends with Jesus? Peter denied they were friends and he felt so guilty he cried. Have you ever done something that made you feel guilty? How did you respond to that feeling? What did you do to make it right? Journal or draw about it below.

6A

Palm Sunday – Coloring Page

Jesus entered the city of Jerusalem riding a donkey. The crowd cheered and shouted, "Hosanna!"

Art: Tatevik Avakyan/Illustration Online LLC

6B

Coded Message – Puzzle

When Jesus rode into the city, a crowd gathered and shouted praises. They shouted a special word. Use the code below to solve the puzzle to find out what the special word is.

_____ _____ _____ _____ _____ _____ _____!

6C

Silly Story – Puzzle

Below you will find the text of today's Bible story, but some of the words are missing. Fill in the blanks with the suggested parts of speech. You can make the words as silly as you'd like!

There was a large crowd gathered in _______ *(noun)*. They were there for a ________ *(noun)*. The crowd heard that _______ *(noun)* was coming to the city too! The crowd took _______ *(plural noun)* and went out to meet Jesus.

The crowd shouted, "_________ *(exclamation)*! Blessings on the one who comes in the name of God! ___________ *(exclamation)* on the king!"

Jesus found a ______ *(noun)* and sat on it as he rode into Jerusalem.

Jesus' friends, the ________ *(plural noun)*, didn't understand what was happening. "Why is Jesus being _______ *(verb)*?" they wondered.

The crowd continued praising Jesus. They wondered what miracles he would do next. The _________ *(plural noun)* were angry. "The whole _____ *(noun)* is following him!" they said to each other.

John 12:12-19

6D

Palm Branch – Art Activity

A crowd gathered as Jesus entered the city of Jerusalem. They put their coats on the road and waved palm branches while they chanted, "Hosanna! Hosanna!"

6E

Holy Week Stones – Storytelling Activity

Palm Sunday is the first day of Holy Week—a time when we remember the life and death of Jesus. Use these symbols to help you remember the events of Holy Week.

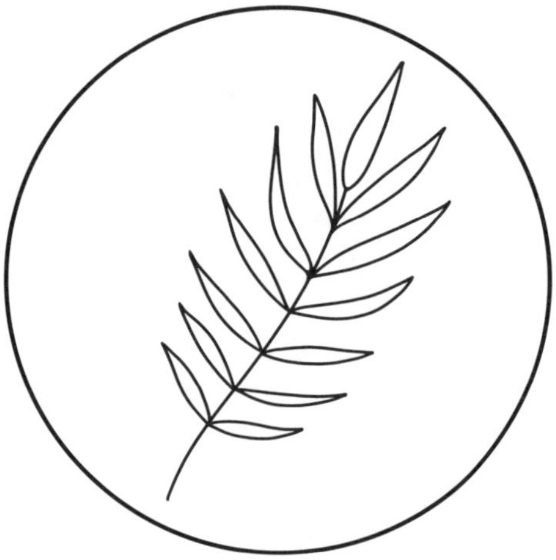

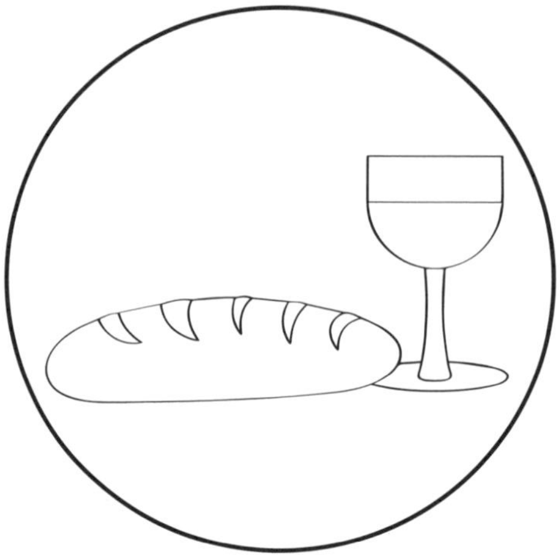

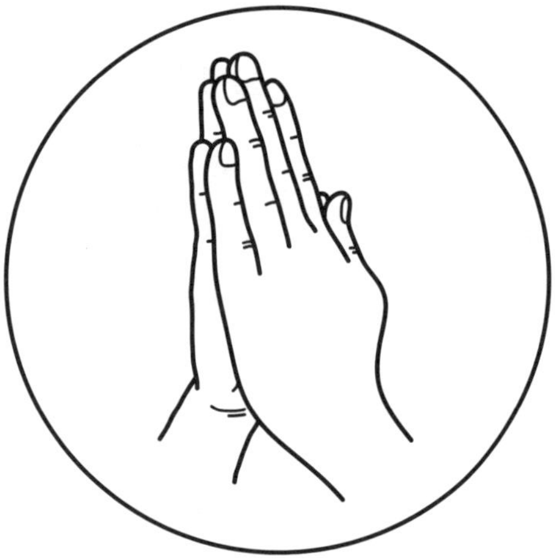

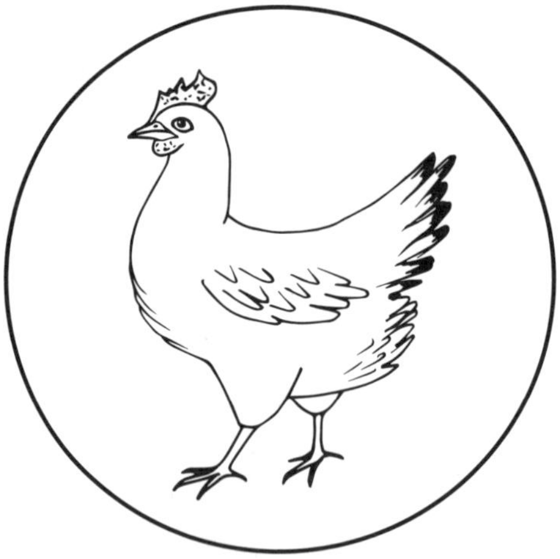

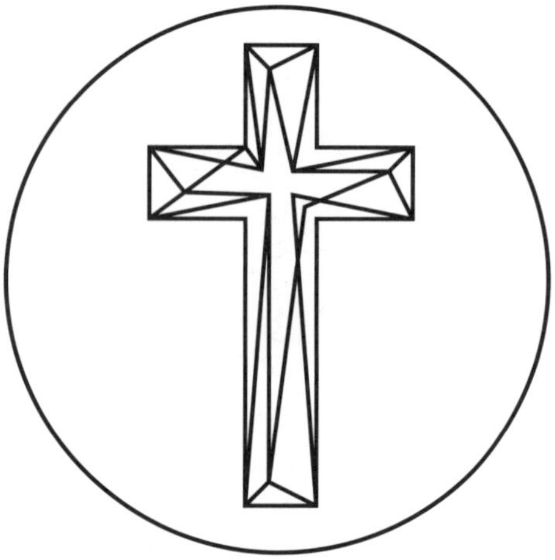

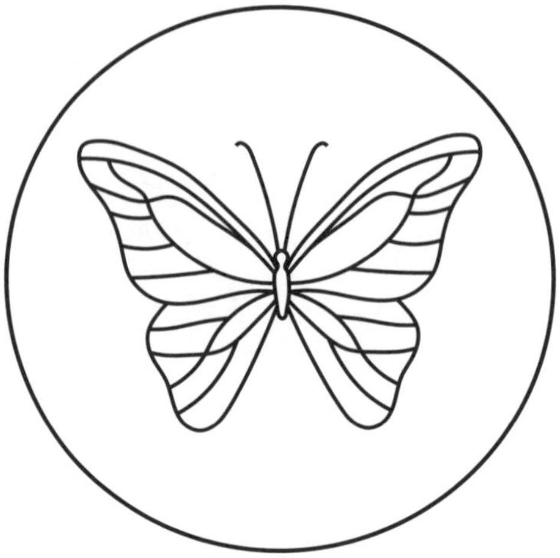

6F

Palm Sunday – Matthew 21:1-11

There was a large crowd gathered in the city of Jerusalem. They were there for a festival called Passover. The crowd heard that Jesus was coming to the city too! The crowd took palm branches and went out to meet Jesus.

The crowd shouted, "Hosanna! Blessings on the one who comes in the name of God! Blessings on the king!"

Jesus found a donkey and sat on it as he rode into Jerusalem.

Jesus' friends, the disciples, didn't understand what was happening. "Why is Jesus being praised?" they wondered.

The crowd continued praising Jesus. They wondered what miracles he would do next. The Pharisees were angry. "The whole world is following him!" they said to each other.

Family Spiritual Practice **Bible Passage:** John 12:12-19

Wonder: After reading the story from the Bible or from the *Celebrate Wonder Bible Storybook*, wonder together. **Ask:** What would you shout if you saw Jesus?

Do: This week can be a hard one! Take time to listen to each other as hard feelings come up.

Pray: Dear God, we turn to you as hard parts of our shared stories feel heavy. Amen.

6G
Holy Week Journaling

This week is an important one for Christians, and it is a hard one to process. We start with Jesus' happy entry into Jerusalem and end with his death on a cross. Take time with God this week to pray and journal about any feelings that come up for you.

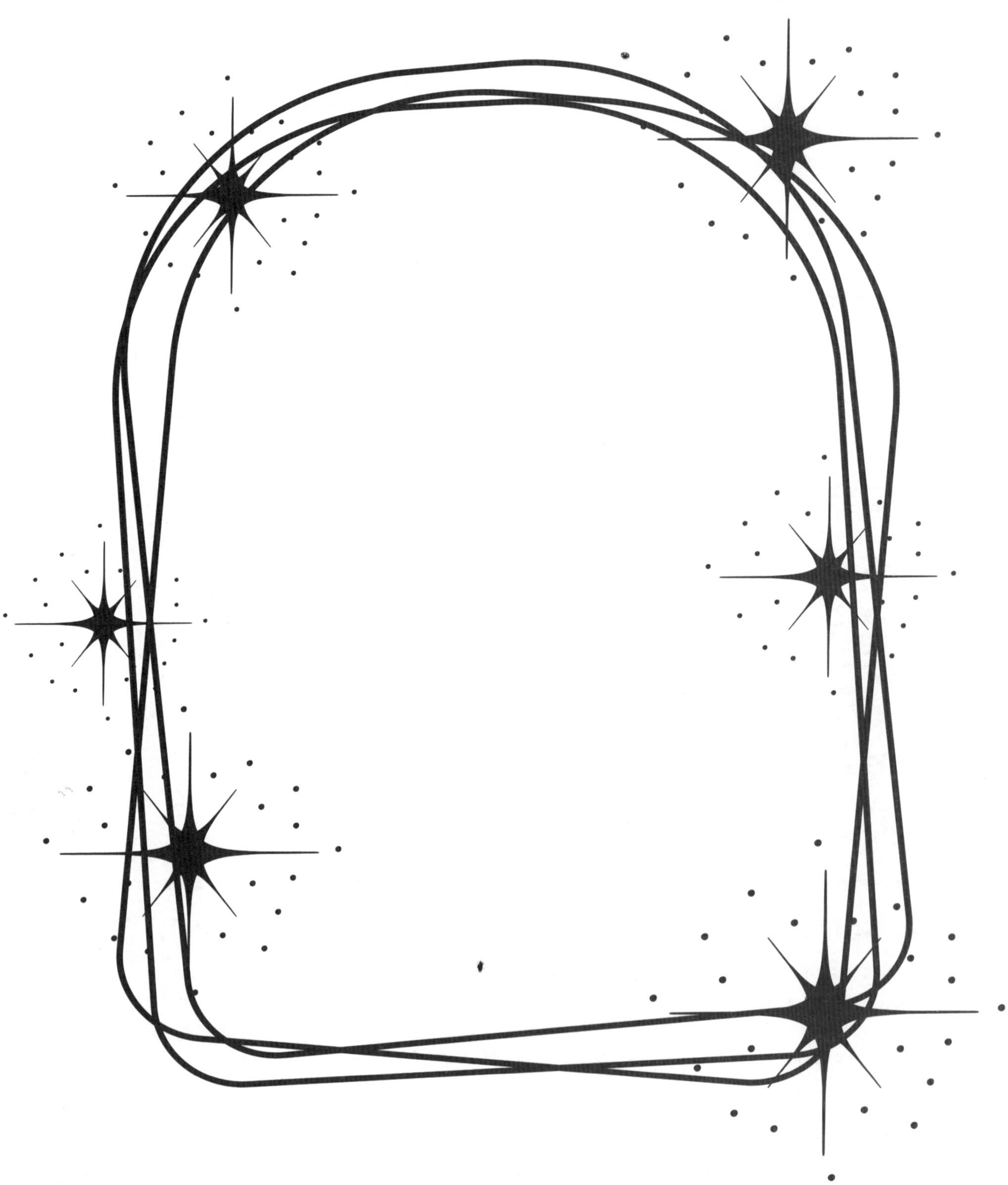

7A

Easter – Coloring Page

Mary Magdalene went to the tomb where Jesus was buried, but when she got to the tomb, Jesus wasn't there. Jesus was alive!

7B

Easter – Coloring Page and Puzzle

Mary Magdalene went to Jesus' tomb to get his body ready to be buried. But when she got to the tomb Jesus wasn't inside! He was alive! Jesus lives. Alleluia! Find the hidden letters to the word Alleluia and then color the page.

Art: Mary Grace Corpus/Gwen Walters

7C

Easter Comic Retelling – Art Activity

The Easter story is one you have probably heard before. Use the comic book below to draw and retell the story.

7D
Empty Tomb – Art Activity

Jesus had been killed on a cross. His body was laid in a tomb. A large stone was rolled over the opening. But when Mary Magdalene came to prepare his body, the stone was rolled away. The tomb was empty. Jesus was alive!

7E

Easter Egg – Art Activity

Eggs are a symbol of new life. When we see an egg, we can remember the new life we get in Jesus.

7F

Easter – John 20:1-18

A long time ago, after Jesus died on the cross, a woman named Mary Magdalene went to the tomb where Jesus had been buried. She went early in the morning on the first day of the week.

Jesus' body had been sealed inside the tomb by a big rock, but when Mary reached the tomb she saw that the large stone had been moved.

Mary ran to tell the disciples, "They have taken Jesus from the tomb and we don't know where they have put him."

Peter and another disciple ran to the tomb to take a look. The disciple who reached the tomb first peeked into the tomb, but Peter went right on in. All Peter saw in the tomb were the linen cloths that Jesus' body was wrapped in.

The disciples returned to where they had been staying, but Mary stood outside the tomb and cried.

Mary looked into the tomb and saw two angels seated where Jesus' body had been.

The angels asked her, "Woman, why are you crying?"

Mary said, "They've taken away Jesus and I don't know where they've put him."

Then Mary turned around and saw Jesus, but she didn't recognize him. She thought he was the gardener.

Jesus said to Mary, "Woman, why are you crying? Who are you looking for?"

Mary said, "Sir, if you have carried Jesus away, tell me where you have put him."

Then Jesus said, "Mary." When Jesus spoke Mary's name, she knew who he was.

Jesus told Mary to go and tell the disciples that he was alive.

Mary went back to the disciples and told them, "I've seen the Lord."

Family Spiritual Practice

Bible Passage: John 20:1-18

Wonder: After reading the story from the Bible or from the *Celebrate Wonder Bible Storybook*, wonder together. **Ask:** What do you think Mary felt in this story?

Do: This week celebrate the new life all around you! Go for a walk and point out all of the new plants and animals.

Pray: Dear God, Jesus is alive! What an amazing miracle! Amen.

7G

Alleluia!

Alleluia! Jesus is alive! What else makes you say alleluia? Draw it below.

8A

Breakfast on the Beach – Coloring Page

One night, Peter and some of Jesus' friends went fishing. In the morning, a man called out to them and invited them to have breakfast on the beach with him. The man was Jesus!

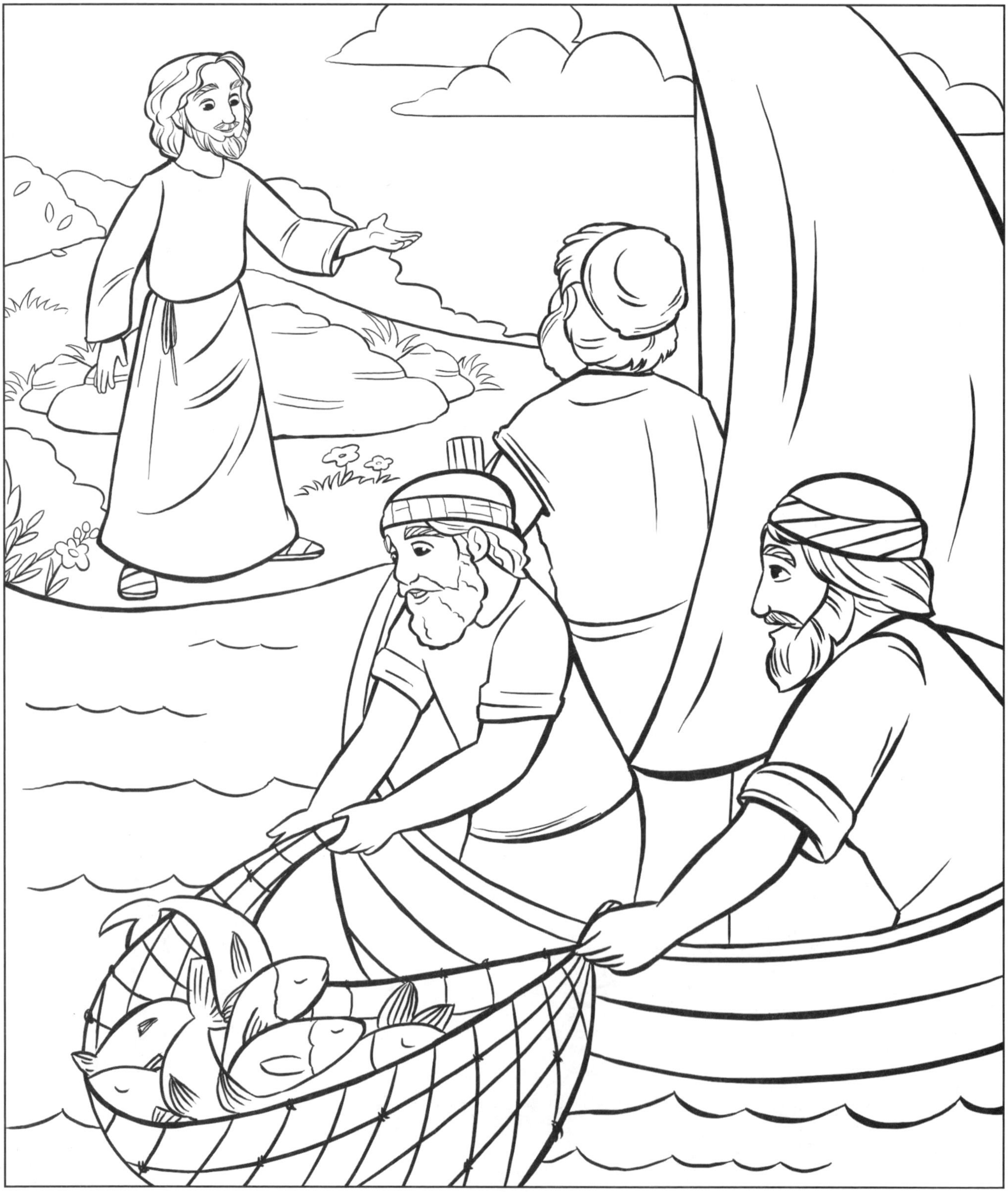

Art: Tatevik Avakyan/Illustration Online LLC

8B

Match the Fish – Puzzle

One night, Peter and some of Jesus' friends went fishing. With Jesus' help, they caught 153 fish! Match the fish on the left side to the fish on the right.

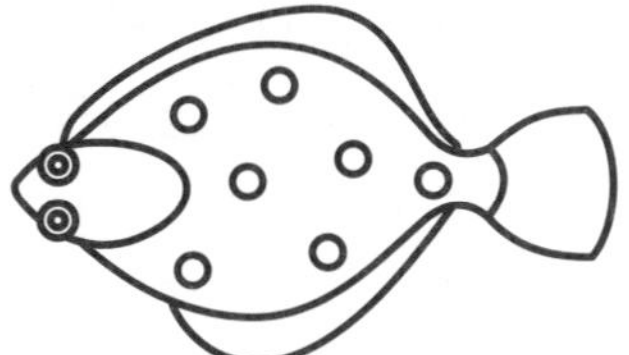

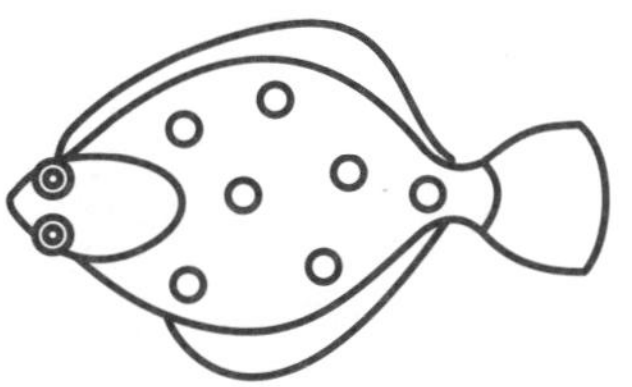

8C

Holy Week Word Search – Puzzle

This month, we learned about Jesus' entry into Jerusalem, Peter's denial, Jesus' death and resurrection, and Jesus' appearance on the beach. Find the hidden words from this month's stories in the puzzle below.

Y	Y	J	A	M	R	B	N	M	Z
L	R	S	U	S	E	J	U	S	R
K	Z	A	J	Z	T	H	P	E	B
C	R	Y	M	P	E	O	T	Y	E
A	V	A	A	Y	P	S	P	E	A
U	H	L	T	M	O	A	E	K	C
L	M	P	I	O	T	N	E	N	H
B	M	N	R	M	W	N	H	O	L
E	A	L	I	V	E	A	S	D	P
B	P	T	A	O	C	H	S	I	F

alive	empty	palm
beach	fish	Peter
coat	hosanna	rooster
cry	Jesus	sheep
donkey	Mary	

8D

April Stars and Constellations – Home Activity

Stars move across the sky and change each season. Constellations and asterisms are star pictures made from groupings of stars. The star pictures below can be found this month by facing south.

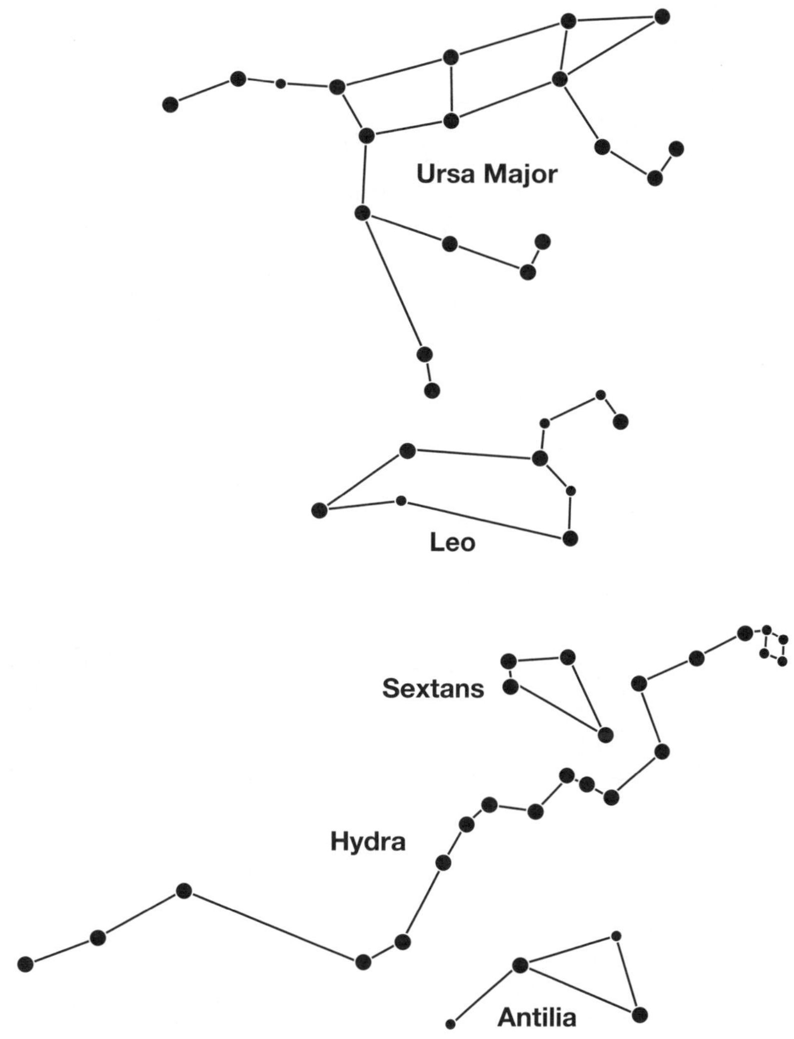

8E

Share the Love – Service Activity

Jesus asked Peter to feed his sheep. Jesus meant that Peter was to share his love with other people. Jesus wants us to share his love with other people too! Use these coupons to share the love with others.

Jesus loves you!

Dear friends, let's love each other, because love is from God.
1 John 4:7

God loves you!

The Lord bless you and protect you. The Lord make his face shine on you and be gracious to you. The Lord lift up his face to you and grant you peace.
Numbers 6:24-26

He will create calm with his love;
he will rejoice over you with singing.
Zephaniah 3:17

8F

Breakfast on the Beach – John 21:1-19

Peter was struggling. He denied knowing Jesus, then Jesus was killed. It broke Peter's heart. Mary Magdalene had showed him that the tomb was empty. Then Jesus appeared to Mary. Jesus was alive! It was a lot to have faith in.

"I am going to go fishing," Peter said to his friends. *Maybe that'll help me feel better.*

"We'll go with you," said the disciples.

The seven men rowed their boat in the sea. It was late in the day as they threw their nets into the water. The friends fished all night, but didn't catch one fish.

As the sun came up, the friends saw a man on the shore. The man called out, "Throw your nets on the other side of the boat."

The friends had already tried that, but they decided to listen to the man. They caught 153 fish in their net!

"It's Jesus!" shouted Peter. He jumped in the water and swam to Jesus.

The friends pulled in the net and brought the boat to shore.

Jesus made them breakfast. They each filled up on bread and fish.

Jesus pulled Peter aside. He knew something was going on with Peter.

"Do you love me, Peter?" asked Jesus.

"Yes, I love you," said Peter.

"Then feed my sheep," said Jesus. "Peter, do you love me?

"Yes," said Peter. His heart was heavy.

"Then feed my sheep," said Jesus. "Peter, do you love me?

"You know I love you, Jesus. You know everything."

"Feed my sheep, Peter," said Jesus.

Family Spiritual Practice **Bible Passage:** John 21:1-19

Wonder: After reading the story from the Bible or from the *Celebrate Wonder Bible Storybook*, wonder together. **Ask:** What do you think Jesus meant when he asked Peter to feed his sheep?

Do: Peter's friends cared for him when he was low. Send a message to a friend this week.

Pray: Dear God, thank you for friends who show us your love. Amen.

8G

Jesus' Friends

In our Bible story, Jesus appears to his friends. Jesus knew how important friends are to life! Who are your best friends? Draw a picture of you with your friends.

9A

Paul is Changed – Coloring Page

Paul was walking to the city of Damascus when all of a sudden he was surrounded by light! Paul heard Jesus' voice and his heart was changed.

9B

Memory Verse Puzzle – Puzzle Activity

This month we will be learning about Paul. He has an encounter with Jesus and begins following Jesus. Paul taught so many people about Jesus and his love.

Right away, he began to preach about Jesus in the synagogues.

9C

Coded Message – Puzzle

In today's Bible story, Paul is changed! He went from hurting followers of Jesus to becoming a follower of Jesus. Solve the coded message below to find out what he did after he changed into a follower of Jesus.

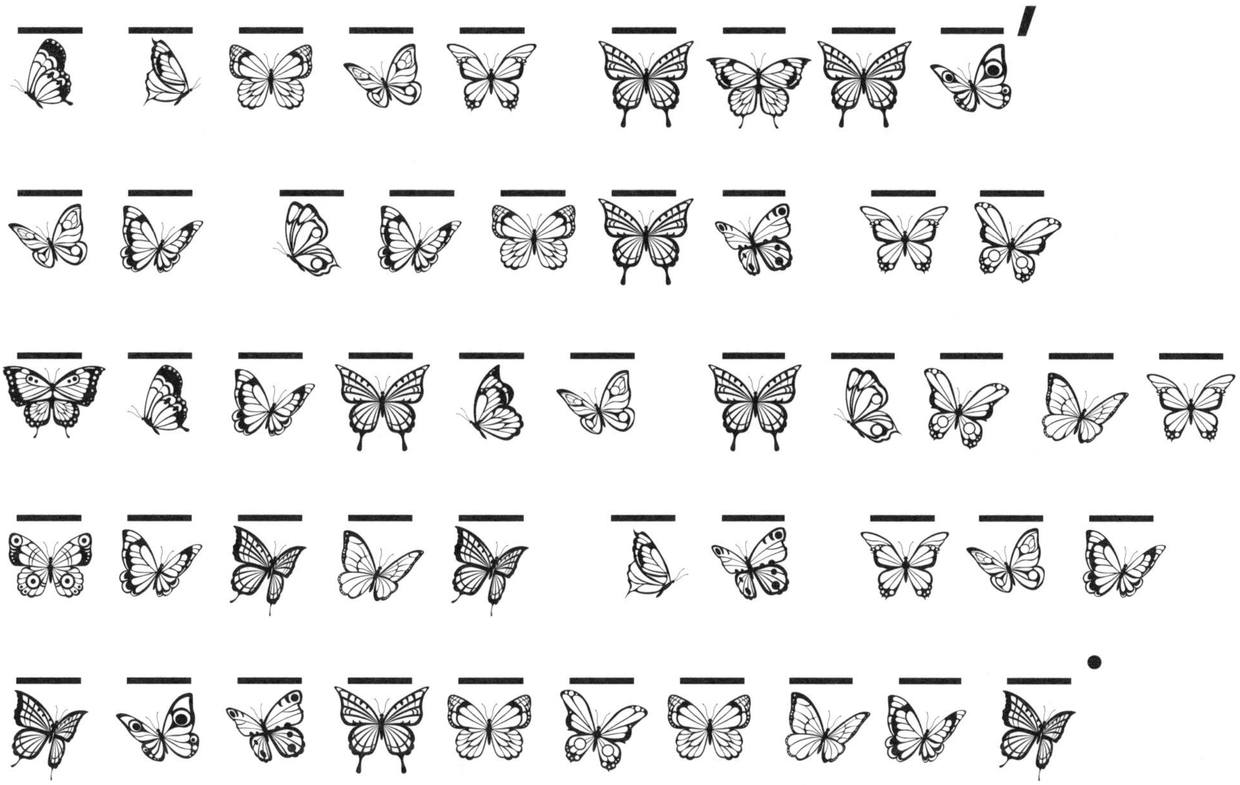

__ __ __ __ __ __ __ __ __,

__ __ __ __ __ __ __ __ __

__ __ __ __ __ __ __ __ __ __ __

__ __ __ __ __ __ __ __ __ __

__ __ __ __ __ __ __ __ __ __.

A B C E G

H I J N O P

R S T U W Y

9D

Proclaim the Good News – Craft Activity

Paul proclaimed the good news about Jesus' love. You can proclaim the good news too. Color the megaphone pattern below. Cut it out. Glue it together to make a megaphone to help you proclaim the good news.

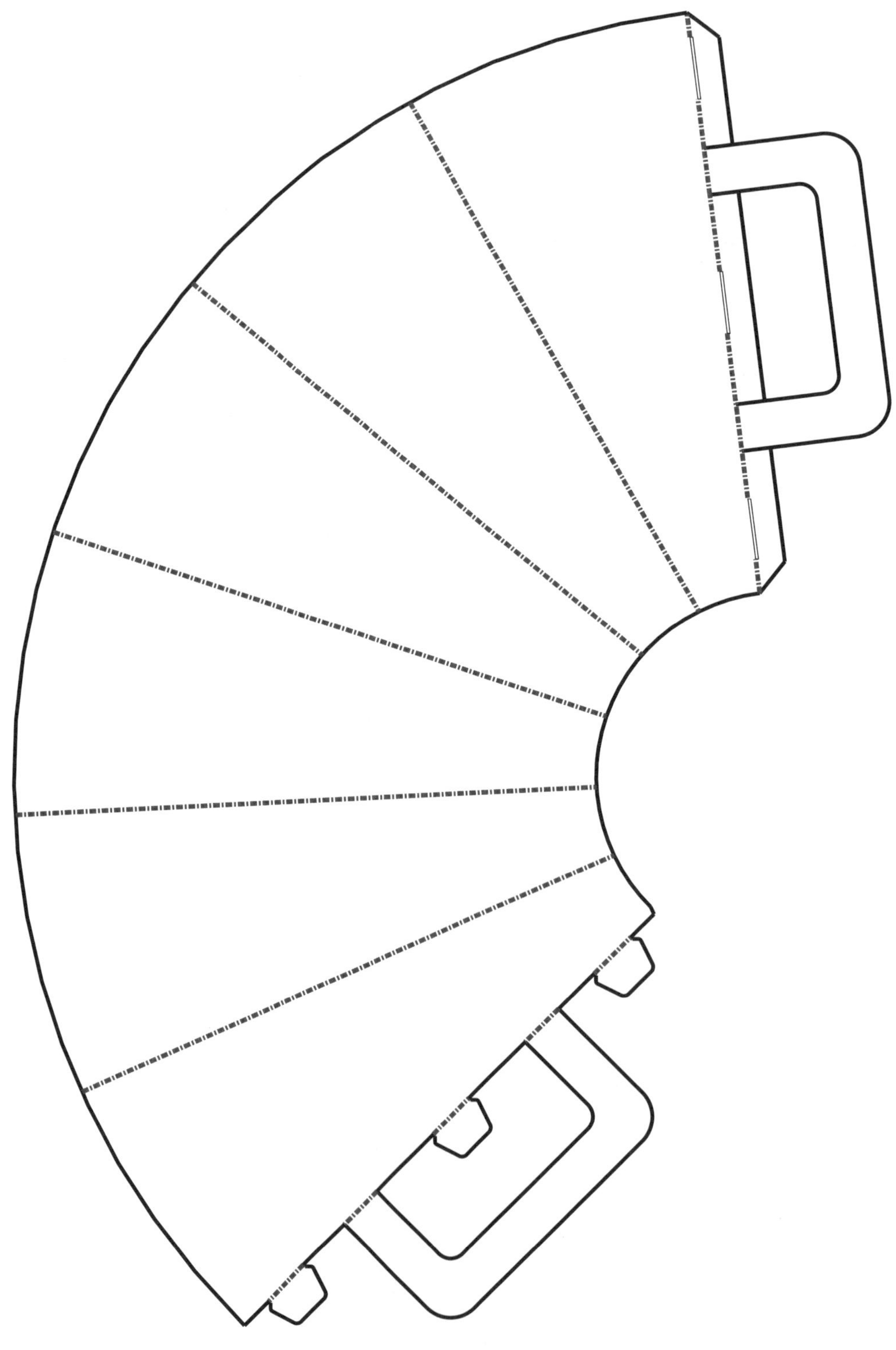

9E

How Have I Changed? – Intergenerational Activity

In our Bible story, Paul changes! He went from hurting Christians to being a leader in the Christian church. That was a big change! All people grow and change. Think about ways you have changed since you were younger. Draw or write about it below.

9F

Paul Is Changed – Acts 9:1-20

Ananias had heard of Paul. Ananias heard Paul had been hurting people who followed Jesus. Ananias and his friends were trying to stay hidden from Paul.

It was a shock when Ananias had a vision of Jesus and Jesus asked him to find Paul.

"Jesus, I have heard that Paul has been hurting your followers. He plans to arrest anyone who believes in you," Ananias said. He wasn't sure he wanted to risk Paul catching him following Jesus.

"Go find Paul, Ananias. I have chosen Paul to share my love with many people outside of our Jewish communities," said Jesus.

Ananais did what he was asked. He went to the house of Judas and there was Paul. Paul couldn't see.

"Hi, Paul. I'm Ananias. Jesus sent me to find you. What happened to you?" said Ananias.

"I was walking down the road. I planned to arrest anyone in the city of Damascus who was following Jesus. But on the way, a great light came over me! I heard the voice of Jesus. He told me to stop hurting him and his followers. Then I lost my vision and I was brought here. I've been here for three days unable to see or eat," said Paul.

"Jesus sent me so you could see again and be baptized," said Ananias.

Instantly, Paul was able to see again. Paul was baptized and right away he began preaching and telling everyone about Jesus.

Family Spiritual Practice **Bible Passage:** Acts 9:1-20

Wonder: After reading the story from the Bible or from the *Celebrate Wonder Bible Storybook*, wonder together. **Ask:** Why do you think Paul was able to change?

Do: Remind each other that you each have a message of love to proclaim. Share your words of love with each other.

Pray: Dear God, thank you for loving us as we grow and change. Amen.

9G

Thank-You Notes

Paul was helped by Ananias. Who has helped you? Draw them a thank-you picture or write a thank you letter.

10A

Paul Escapes with Help – Coloring Page

Paul wanted to help spread Jesus' message of love, but people still didn't trust him. Paul had to get help from some friends to escape a dangerous situation!

Art: Tatevik Avakyan/Illustration Online LLC

10B

Missing Vowels – Puzzle

Paul spent his whole ministry sharing the message of Jesus' life and love. We can do that too! Solve the puzzle to find out what that is called.

P R _ C L _ _ M _ N G

G _ D´S W _ R D

A1	E0	I2	O3	U0

10C

Paul Escapes Anagram – Puzzle

In today's story, Paul proclaims Jesus' message of love, but some people still don't trust him. He has to get some help from his friends to stay safe. Use the letters from the words "proclaim" and "friends" to make new words.

PROCLAIM

FRIENDS

10D

What Makes a Good Friend? – Journaling Activity

Friends help us have fun, grow into whom God created us to be, and support us when things get hard. What else makes a good friend? Is there someone in your life that you call a good friend? Write or draw about them below.

10E

Find Your Match – Game Activity

We all need help from friends sometimes. Look for your matching friend in this game.

10F

Paul Escapes with Help – Acts 9:21-25

Some friends of Paul were with him in the city of Damascus. They listened to Paul proclaim that Jesus is God's Son. They listened to Paul proclaim that Jesus was the savior. The friends were inspired by Paul's change.

But there were other people in Damascus who were confused by Paul's change.

"Wasn't Paul coming here to arrest the followers of Jesus? Now, he's proclaiming that we should all follow Jesus," said one of the people.

"Do you think he's trying to trick us so we will get in trouble?" asked another person.

"I don't think we should trust him. Maybe we need to hurt him before he can hurt us," suggested another person.

Paul's friends heard the plan to hurt him. They came up with a plan to help him escape Damascus, so Paul wouldn't get hurt.

The friends found a large basket and some long rope. They put Paul in the basket and lowered him over the wall of the city.

Paul was safe!

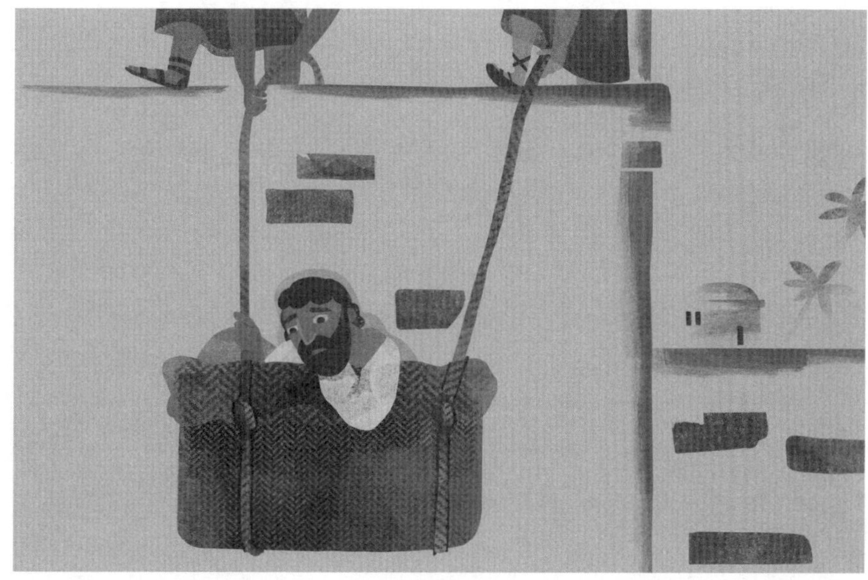

Family Spiritual Practice

Bible Passage: Acts 9:21-25

Wonder: After reading the story from the Bible or from the *Celebrate Wonder Bible Storybook*, wonder together. **Ask:** What makes a good friend?

Do: Reach out to one of your family friends this week and catch up. If there is a way to help one another, spend time doing that.

Pray: Dear God, thank you for friends who love us well. Amen.

10G

Your Voice Matters

We've been learning about Paul and the message he proclaimed about Jesus' love. Paul's voice mattered, and your voice matters! What message do you feel led to share with your family, your friends, and your community? Write or draw it below.

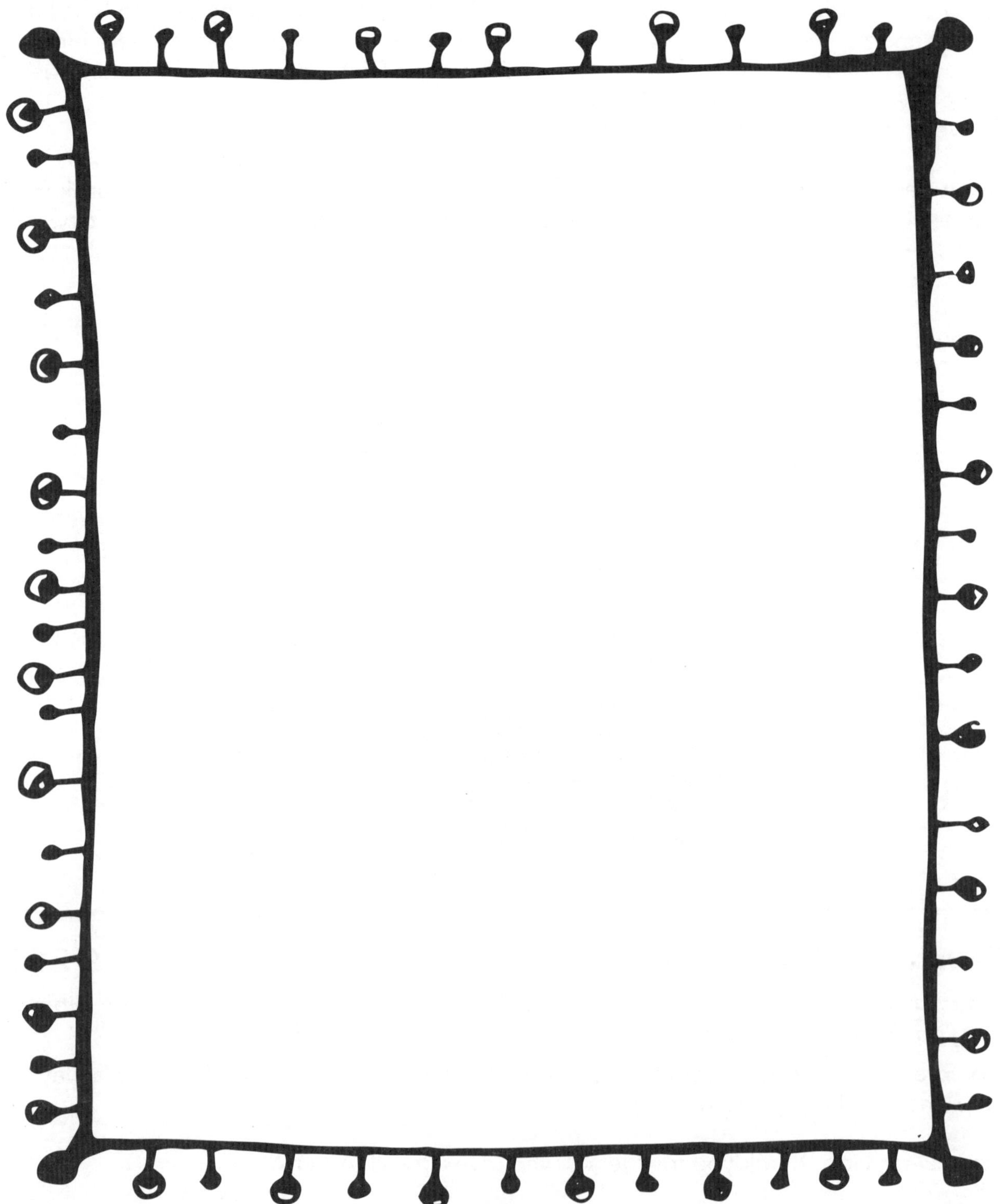

11A

Paul and Timothy – Coloring Page

Paul met Timothy when Timothy was a young boy. Timothy became a follower of Jesus and a leader in the church.

11B

What's Silly With This Picture? – Puzzle and Coloring Page

Paul met Timothy when Timothy was a young boy. Timothy became a follower of Jesus and a leader in the church. But there are some silly things in this picture of Paul and Timothy. Can you find and circle them all? Then color the picture.

11C

People in This Month's Stories – Puzzle

This month we are hearing stories about Paul and the people who helped him along the way. Solve the crossword puzzle below using the names in the box from this month's stories.

Word Bank:

PAUL	TIMOTHY
JESUS	SILAS
ANANIAS	JAILER
FRIENDS	SAILORS
FOLLOWERS	PRISONERS

11D

Who Teaches You About God? – Art Activity

Timothy's mother and grandmother taught him about God. Who teaches you about God? Draw a portrait of the people who teach you below.

11E

Inherited Traits – Science Activity

For each trait listed below, take a survey of your class and discover how many people fit in each category.

Eye Color																			
Blue																			
Brown																			
Green																			
Hazel																			
Other																			
Hair Color																			
Black																			
Blond																			
Brown																			
Red																			
Other																			
Earlobes																			
Attached																			
Not Attached																			
Ability to Curl Tongue																			
Yes																			
No																			
Hairline																			
Forms a point																			
Straight across																			

11F

Paul and Timothy – Acts 16:1-5; 2 Timothy 1:5-7

Timothy grew up in a town called Lystra with his mom, dad, and grandmother. His mom and grandmother taught him stories about God.

When Timothy was a boy, Paul travelled to Lystra to proclaim Jesus' message of love. Paul was impressed by Timothy's leadership skills and Timothy's love for God. Paul trained Timothy to go out and start a new church in a town called Ephesus.

While Timothy was proclaiming Jesus' message of love, he started to feel sad. He needed some cheering up and some encouragement to continue proclaiming the good news.

Paul sent Timothy a letter. Paul said, "Dear Timothy, I am thankful to God. It is such a blessing to serve God. I am praying for you all the time because I know you are sad. I hope you will feel happy soon. I know you have a strong faith in God, Timothy. Your mother and your grandmother taught you about God's love and how to be a faithful follower of Jesus. Remember that you have special gifts to share with people. God gave you a strong, loving spirit."

This letter from Paul made Timothy feel better.

Family Spiritual Practice **Bible Passage:** Acts 16:1-5; 2 Timothy 1:5-7

Wonder: After reading the story from the Bible or from the *Celebrate Wonder Bible Storybook*, wonder together. **Ask:** What makes a good friend?

Do: Do you know someone that could use encouragement? Send a card or letter reminding that person that they are loved.

Pray: Dear God, thank you for friends who encourage us. Amen.

11G

Who Cheers You Up?

When you are sad, who do you turn to for cheering up? Draw a portrait of that person or animal.

12A

Paul and Silas in Prison – Coloring Page

Paul and Silas traveled together to proclaim Jesus' message of love. There were some people who didn't like their message, so they were put in jail. What do you think happened next?

12B

Songs of Praise – Matching Puzzle

Paul and Silas were arrested and put in prison. That didn't stop them from proclaiming Jesus' message of love through songs of praise. Match the musical notes on the left with the ones on the right.

12C

Missing Memory Verse Vowels – Puzzle

This month we have been learning a memory verse about proclaiming. Add the vowels back into the words to solve the puzzle and read the memory verse.

"TH_S_ P_ _PL_ _R_

S_RV_NTS _F TH_ M_ST

H_GH G_D! TH_Y _R_

PR_CL_ _M_NG _ W_Y _F

S_LV_T_ _N T_ Y_ _!"

_CTS 16:1

A9	E9	I4	O9	U1

12D
Proclaiming Jesus' Message – Reflection Activity

Paul and Silas proclaimed Jesus' message of love. This was the most important message to them. What is the most important message to you? Reflect on what cause you want to tell others about and write or draw your message below.

12E

Song of Praise – Intergenerational Activity

In our Bible story, Paul and Silas sing songs of praise as a way to proclaim Jesus' message of love. Sing the song below together as a way of doing the same.

Tell Somebody (Spring 2021, Unit 2: Share)

The first light of the new week dawned,
not a whole lot was going on.
Until the earth shook up and an angel came
with lightning—frightening.

Two good women heard him say,
"This ain't the time to be afraid.
That man, Jesus, quit the grave,
and now is the time to celebrate.
Go out and tell somebody."

I'm gonna tell somebody.
I'm gonna tell somebody 'bout it.
I'm gonna tell somebody.
I'm gonna tell somebody 'bout it.

Jesus rose and walked around;
friends that saw him hit the ground.
He said, "Tell everybody how I lived,
like how to love and how to give."

So, on the way to church one day,
they healed a man in Jesus' name.
The man jumped up when they told him, "Rise,"
and nobody could believe their eyes.
They had to tell somebody.

I'm gonna tell somebody.
I'm gonna tell somebody 'bout it.
I'm gonna tell somebody.
I'm gonna tell somebody 'bout it.

When we put our hearts together,
we treat each other even better.
That's what love is all about.
It just makes me wanna go out . . .

I'm gonna tell somebody.
I'm gonna tell somebody 'bout it.
I'm gonna tell somebody.
I'm gonna tell somebody 'bout it.

I'm gonna tell somebody.
I'm gonna tell somebody 'bout it.
I'm gonna tell somebody.
I'm gonna tell somebody 'bout it.

I'm gonna tell somebody.
I'm gonna tell somebody 'bout it.
I'm gonna tell somebody.
I'm gonna tell somebody 'bout it.

Written by Derek Webb &
Abbie Parker

12F

Paul and Silas in Prison – Acts 16:16-40

Silas was asked to travel with Paul. Silas agreed and went to several places, including the town of Philippi.

While Paul and Silas were in Philippi, they met a woman who had been enslaved. She was being forced to predict the future for people by the people who owned her.

While Silas and Paul were walking through town the woman shouted at them, "These people are servants of the Most High God! They are proclaiming a way of salvation to you!"

Silas kept quiet while she shouted at them, but it was starting to bother Paul. Silas listened as Paul said, "You're free to stop predicting futures!"

Just like that, the woman was healed and was no longer able to predict the future.

But this made her owners angry. They had Silas and Paul arrested and taken to prison.

While they were locked in prison, Silas and Paul sang songs of praise to God while the others in jail listened. All of a sudden, an earthquake shook the prion and all of the prison doors opened! The people in the prison could have escaped, but they didn't.

When the jailer realized all of the prison doors had opened, he got worried the people had all escaped. He ran to see if the people were still there. They were! This surprised the jailer.

"Don't worry, we're all here!" said Paul.

"You're honorable people. What must I do to be like you?" asked the jailer.

"You should believe in Jesus and be baptized," said Silas and Paul.

"Come home with me and baptize my whole family," said the jailer.

Silas and Paul went home with the jailer and baptized his whole family.

Family Spiritual Practice

Bible Passage: Acts 16:16-40

Wonder: After reading the story from the Bible or from the *Celebrate Wonder Bible Storybook*, wonder together. **Ask:** What can we learn from this story?

Do: This week, choose an issue to support as a family. Then proclaim Jesus' message of love through advocacy and service.

Pray: Dear God, help us proclaim your love through the actions we take. Amen.

12G

Actions Proclaim

Paul and Silas surprised the jailer. Instead of escaping, Paul and Silas stayed. This action made the jailer trust them. What we do tells others about us, too. What do your actions say about who you are? Write or draw about it below.

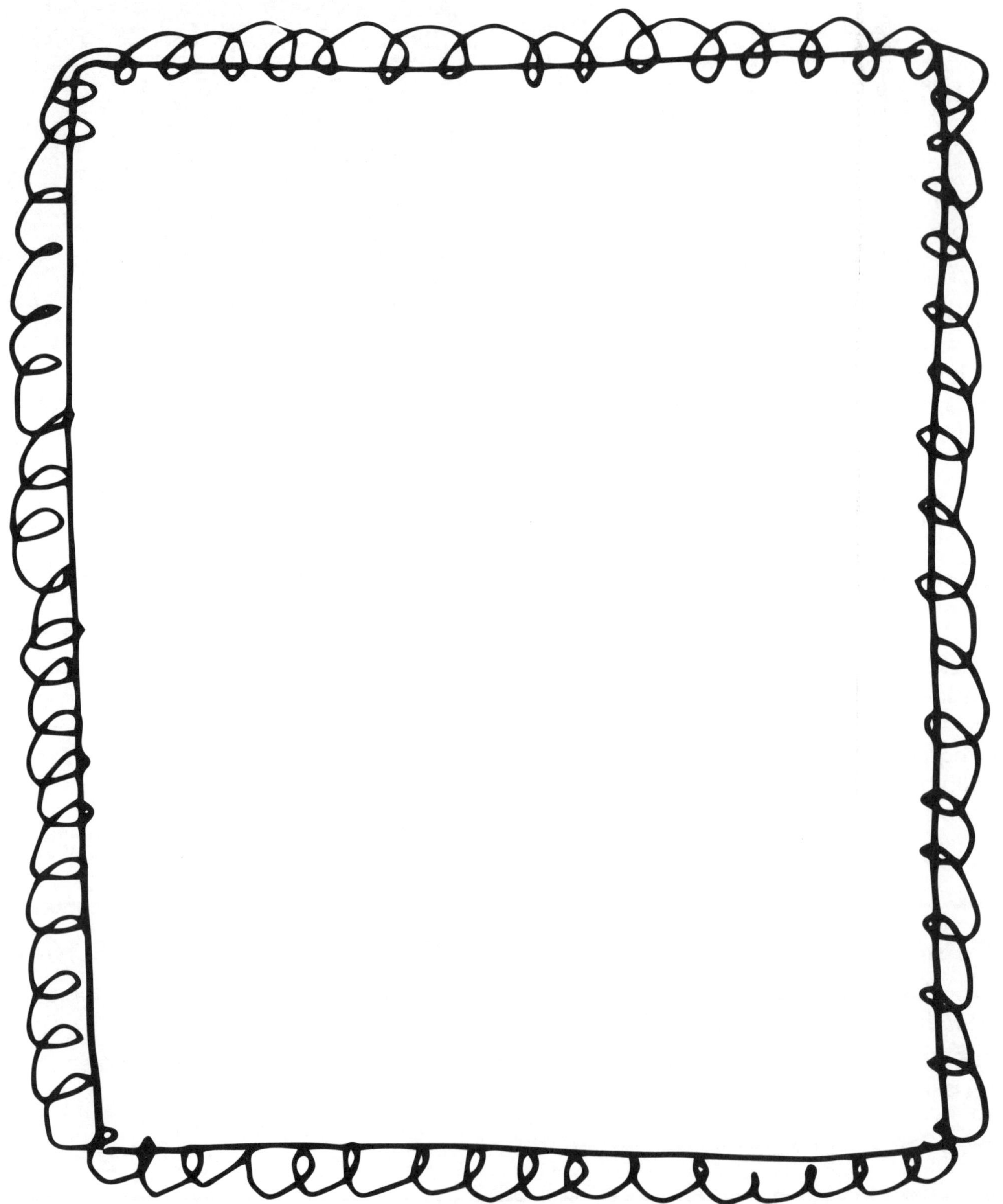

13A

Shipwrecked – Coloring Page

Paul was arrested. As a Roman citizen, he was allowed to ask to be taken to the city of Rome for his trial. He had to get on a ship to sail to Rome. While on the ship, the boat was in a shipwreck!

13B

Sailing to Rome – Maze

Paul was arrested. As a Roman citizen, he was allowed to ask to be taken to the city of Rome for his trial. He had to get on a ship to sail to Rome. Solve the maze to help Paul get to Rome.

Art: Ralph Voltz/Illustration Online LLC

13C

Paul Word Search – Puzzle

This month, we learned a lot about Paul and the meassge of Jesus' love he proclaimed with the help of friends. Use the word bank below to find and circle words from this month's stories.

Y	L	E	A	D	E	R	S	K	T
H	H	G	Y	E	J	A	W	I	Y
M	Q	T	T	G	I	E	M	I	F
T	I	X	I	N	N	O	S	R	W
E	S	A	A	A	T	W	I	U	L
K	P	N	L	H	F	E	Z	T	S
S	A	A	Y	C	N	B	G	O	V
A	L	T	C	D	O	L	U	A	P
B	B	D	S	S	N	R	C	V	K
L	I	G	H	T	E	A	P	G	Q

Ananias	Faith	Light
Basket	Friends	Paul
Changed	Jesus	Proclaim
Escape	Leader	Timothy

13D

May Stars and Constellations – Home Activity

Stars move across the sky and change each season. Constellations and asterisms are star pictures made from groupings of stars. The star pictures below can be found this month by facing south.

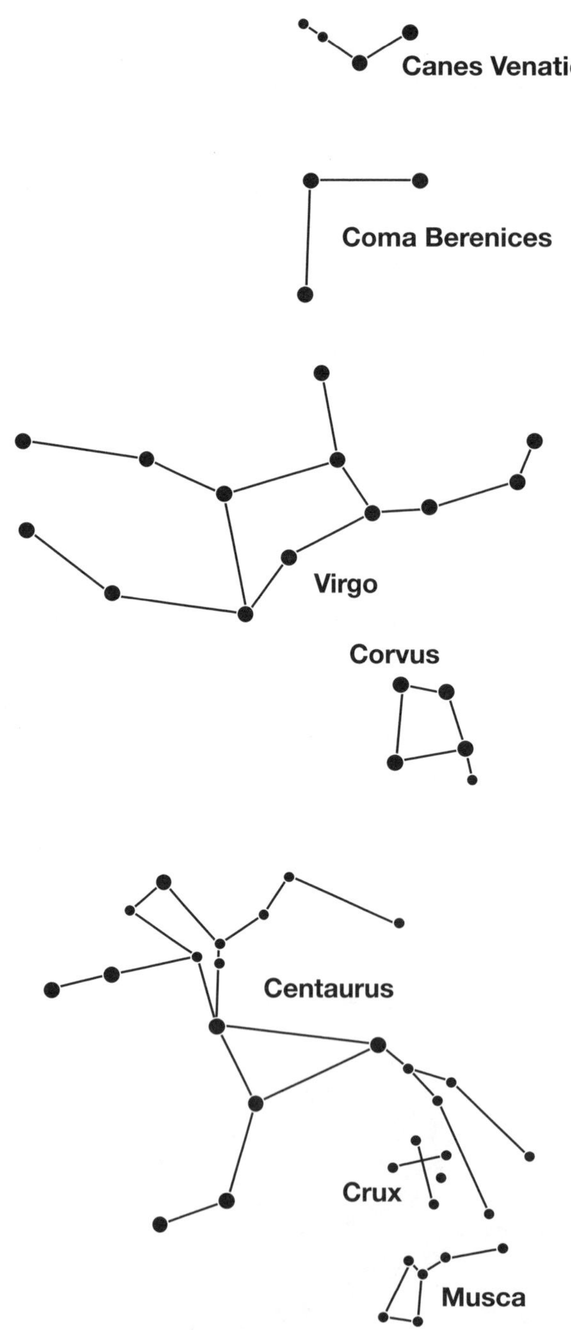

13E

Paul Review – Intergenerational Activity

Make copies of this quiz for all participants and have them review the stories through taking the quiz. Consider pairing your youngest children with the adults in your group.

What did Paul want to do to the people who followed Jesus? 1. Give them presents 2. Put them in jail 3. Throw a party 4. Have a picnic	A voice came from the light and spoke to Paul. This voice was _______. 1. Jesus 2. Elijah 3. Barnabas 4. Carl	What happened to Paul when he saw the bright light? 1. He could see 2. He got a sunburn 3. He became blind 4. He bought sunglasses
After Paul's eyes were opened, Paul began doing what? 1. Singing professionally 2. Making glasses 3. Dancing in the streets 4. Preaching in the synagogues	When Paul found out people wanted to hurt him, Paul decided to do what? 1. Fight back 2. Leave the city 3. Call his mom 4. Write a book	True or False: Paul needed help from his friends, but he couldn't find anyone to help him. Paul's friends helped Paul escape by putting him in ______. 1. A basket 2. A fast car 3. A barrel 4. A closet
Paul met Timothy in... 1. Jerusalem 2. Lystra 3. Damascus 4. Nazareth	Timothy learned about God and Jesus from... 1. A circus clown 2. A magazine 3. His mother and grandmother 4. A TikTok video	Paul shipwrecked on the way to... 1. His trial in Rome 2. A concert on an island 3. His birthday party 4. Church

13F

Shipwrecked – Acts 27:1-44

Paul was in prison because some of the Jewish leaders were not happy with his missionary work. Paul was being sent to Rome so the Emperor of the Roman Empire could hear the case against him. However, the journey to Rome didn't go as planned.

After the ship sailed, they encountered delays and weren't able to travel as quickly as they hoped. The weather was getting bad. Paul was an experienced sailor, and he warned the ship's captain and crew that if they continued to travel there would be damage to the ship and some people would lose their lives.

The captain decided to sail on anyway. Pretty soon they encountered a fierce storm with really strong winds. After several days the ship had been so battered by the storm that the crew began to throw cargo overboard. They were trying to lighten the load on the ship so it wouldn't fall apart.

After a few more days, when the storm was still going strong, the crew gave up hope that any of them would live through the storm.

Paul told the crew and other passengers that an angel from God had visited him and told him that he would make it to Rome

because God had work for him to do there. Paul encouraged the crew and passengers and told them to have courage and not give up! Paul said they would all be saved but they needed to park their ship on an island because the ship was not going to make it.

The ship fell apart but Paul and the entire crew and all the other passengers were able to swim to the island and be saved. Paul not only had courage himself, but he was able to help the rest of the people have courage, too.

Family Spiritual Practice

Bible Passage: Acts 27:1-44

Wonder: After reading the story from the Bible or from the *Celebrate Wonder Bible Storybook*, wonder together. **Ask:** What would you have done if you were on the ship?

Do: Paul and the people on the boat prayed and ate to prepare for the shipwreck. What do you do to prepare when something hard is getting ready to happen?

Pray: Dear God, help us proclaim your love through the words we say. Amen.

13G

Spring Stories

You have heard a lot of amazing stories this spring—from Jesus' ministry, resurrection and appearance, to Paul's ministry. Which story stands out to you? Retell the story through words or drawings below.

Answer Key

1B

2B

2C

3B

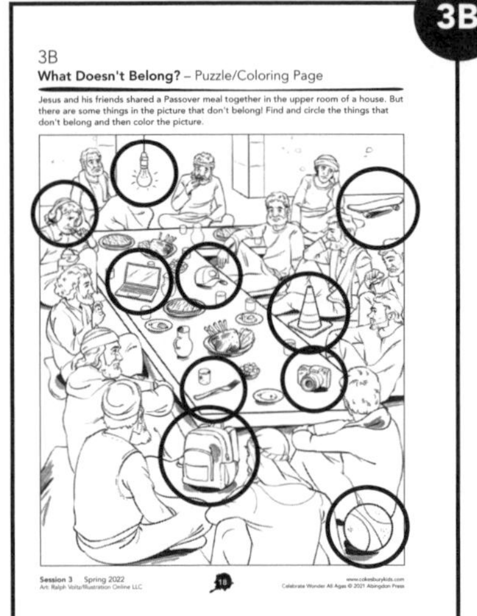

3C

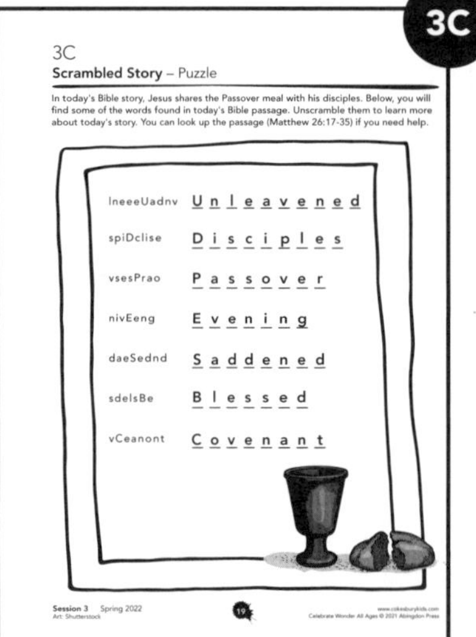

4B

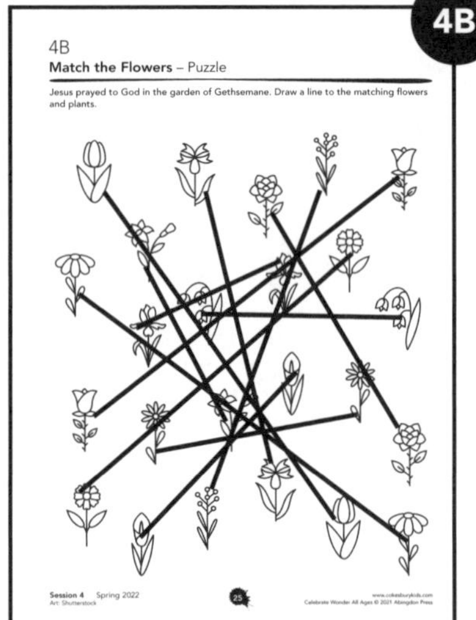

4C

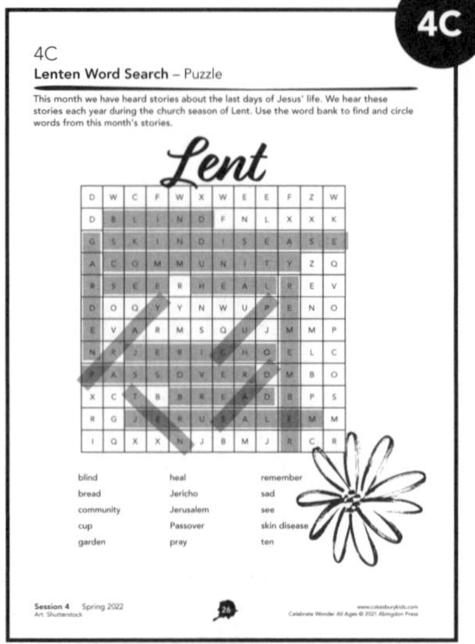

Answer Key

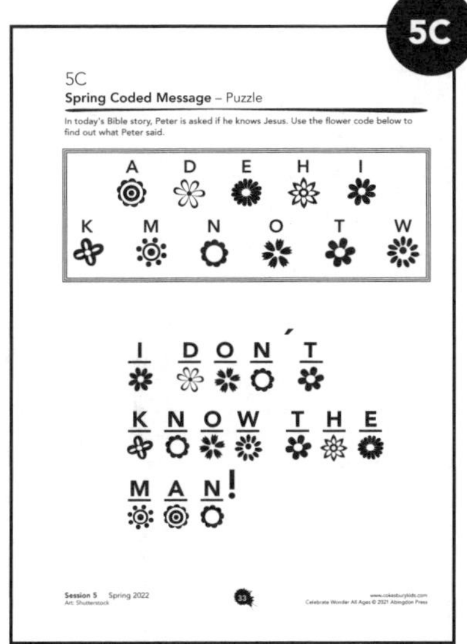
5C
5C
Spring Coded Message – Puzzle
In today's Bible story, Peter is asked if he knows Jesus. Use the flower code below to find out what Peter said.
A D E H I
K M N O T W
I DON'T
KNOW THE
MAN!

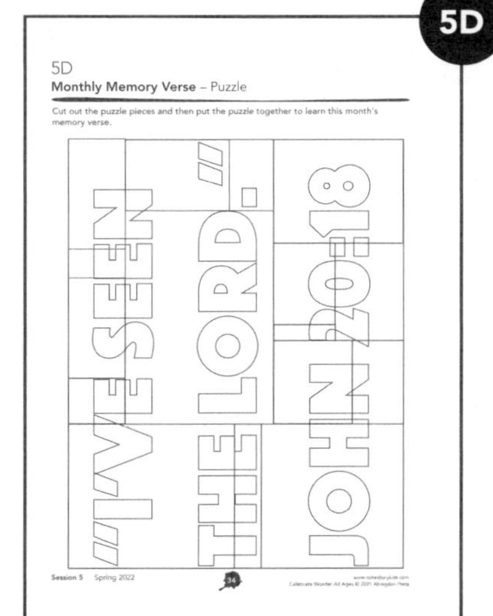
5D
5D
Monthly Memory Verse – Puzzle
Cut out the puzzle pieces and then put the puzzle together to learn this month's memory verse.
"I'VE SEEN
THE LORD."
JOHN 20:18

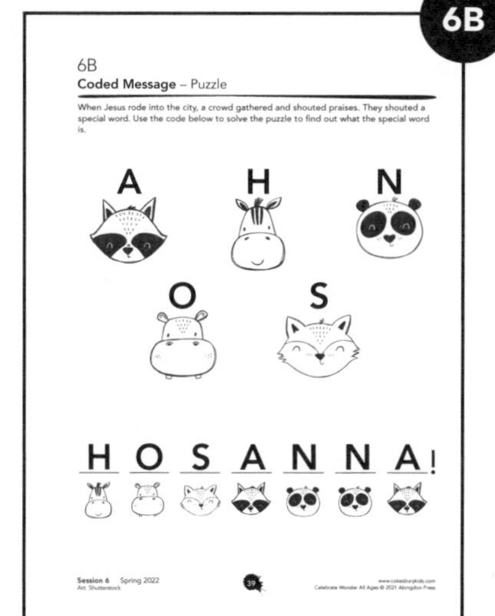
6B
6B
Coded Message – Puzzle
When Jesus rode into the city, a crowd gathered and shouted praises. They shouted a special word. Use the code below to solve the puzzle to find out what the special word is.
A H N
O S
HOSANNA!

7B
7B
Easter – Coloring Page and Puzzle
Mary Magdalene went to Jesus' tomb to get his body ready to be buried. But when she got to the tomb Jesus wasn't inside! He was alive! Jesus lives. Alleluia! Find the hidden letters to the word Alleluia and then color the page.

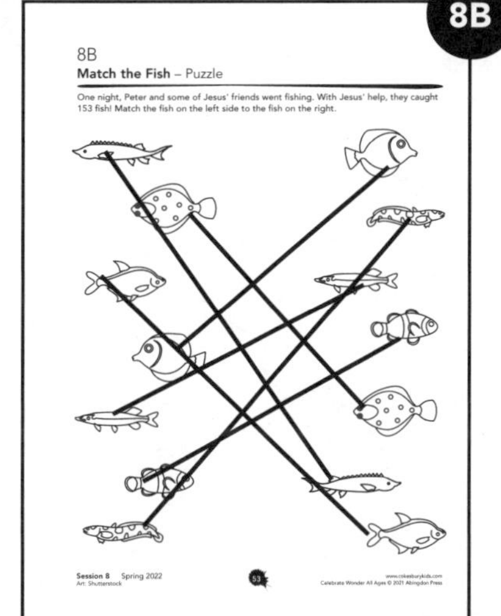
8B
8B
Match the Fish – Puzzle
One night, Peter and some of Jesus' friends went fishing. With Jesus' help, they caught 153 fish! Match the fish on the left side to the fish on the right.

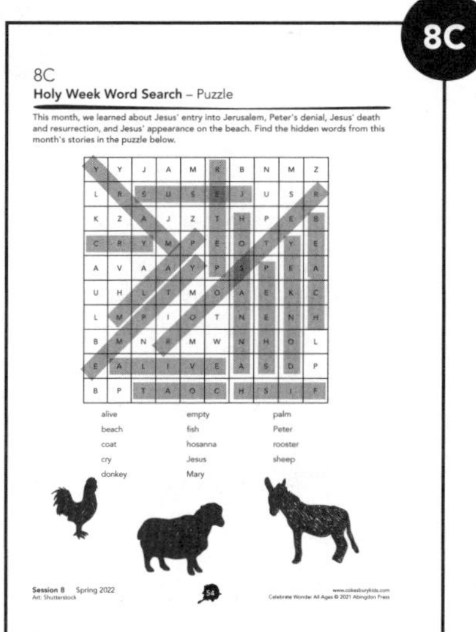
8C
8C
Holy Week Word Search – Puzzle
This month, we learned about Jesus' entry into Jerusalem, Peter's denial, Jesus' death and resurrection, and Jesus' appearance on the beach. Find the hidden words from this month's stories in the puzzle below.
alive
beach
coat
cry
donkey
empty
fish
hosanna
Jesus
Mary
palm
Peter
rooster
sheep

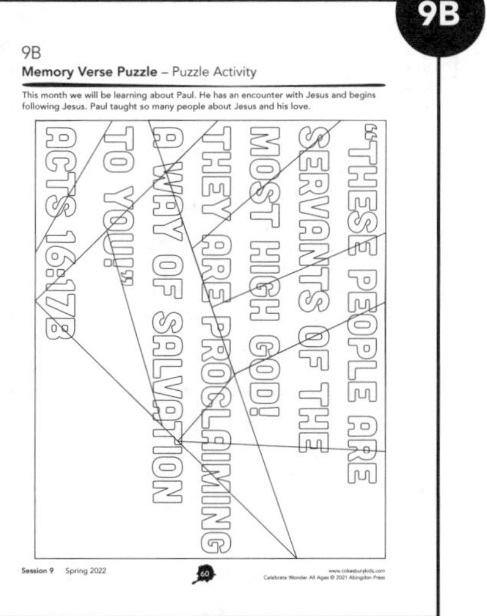
9B
9B
Memory Verse Puzzle – Puzzle Activity
This month we will be learning about Paul. He has an encounter with Jesus and begins following Jesus. Paul taught so many people about Jesus and his love.
"THESE PEOPLE ARE
SERVANTS OF THE
MOST HIGH GOD!
THEY ARE PROCLAIMING
A WAY OF SALVATION
TO YOU!"
ACTS 16:17B

Answer Key

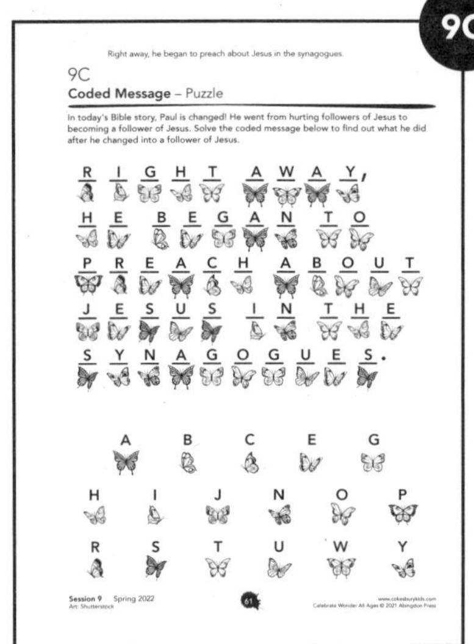
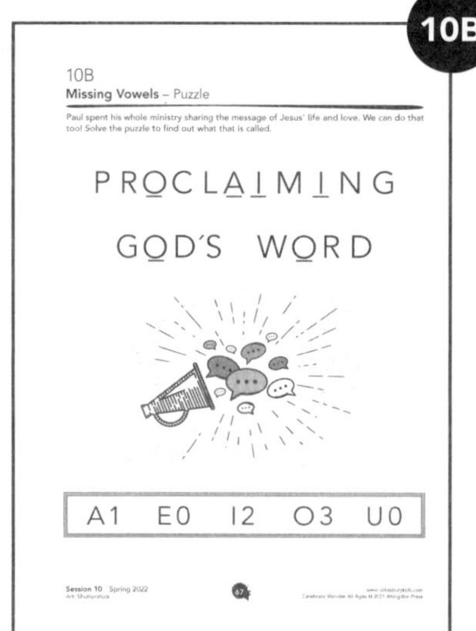
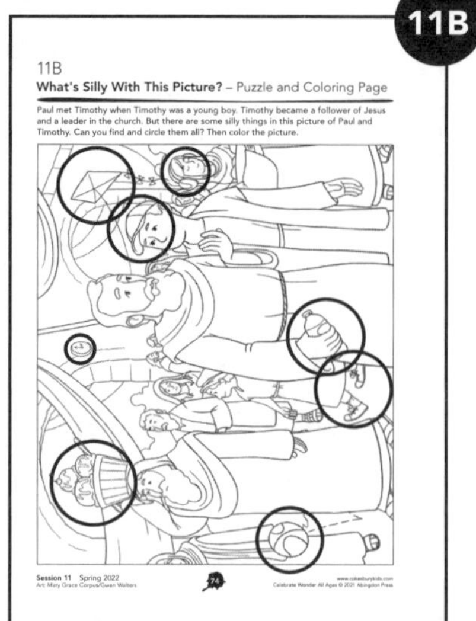

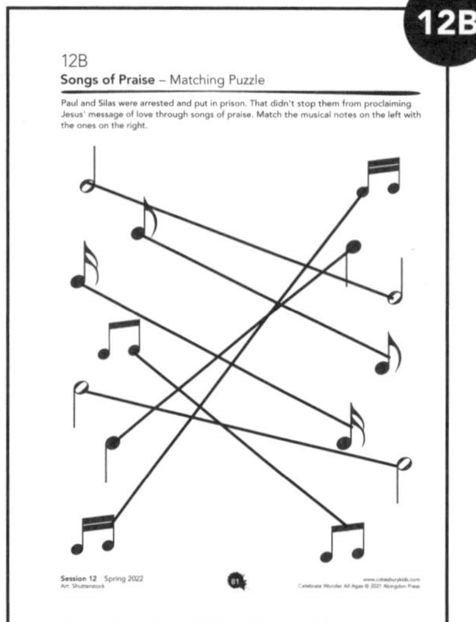
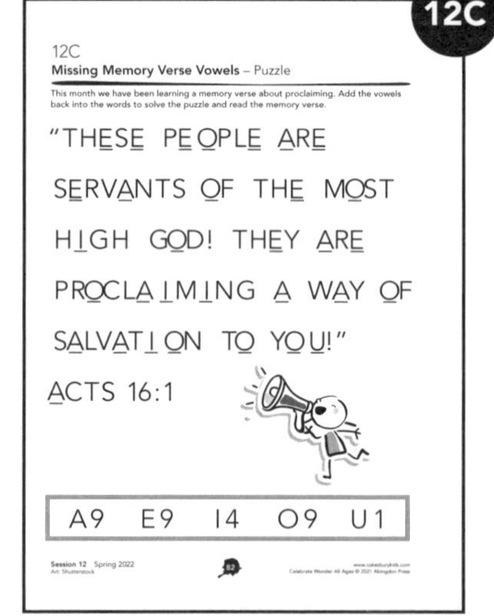

Spring 2022